MAD LIBS®

MAD ABOUT MAD LIBS

concept created by Roger Price and Leonard Stern

PSS!
PRICE STERN SLOAN
An Imprint of Penguin Group (USA) Inc.

PRICE STERN SLOAN
Published by the Penguin Group
Penguin Group (USA) Inc., 375 Hudson Street, New York, New York 10014, USA
Penguin Group (Canada), 90 Eglinton Avenue East, Suite 700, Toronto, Ontario M4P 2Y3, Canada
(a division of Pearson Penguin Canada Inc.)
Penguin Books Ltd, 80 Strand, London WC2R 0RL, England
Penguin Ireland, 25 St Stephen's Green, Dublin 2, Ireland (a division of Penguin Books Ltd)
Penguin Group (Australia), 707 Collins Street, Melbourne, Victoria 3008, Australia
(a division of Pearson Australia Group Pty Ltd)
Penguin Books India Pvt Ltd, 11 Community Centre, Panchsheel Park, New Delhi—110 017, India
Penguin Group (NZ), 67 Apollo Drive, Rosedale, Auckland 0632, New Zealand
(a division of Pearson New Zealand Ltd)
Penguin Books (South Africa), Rosebank Office Park, 181 Jan Smuts Avenue,
Parktown North 2193, South Africa
Penguin China, B7 Jiaming Center, 27 East Third Ring Road North,
Chaoyang District, Beijing 100020, China

Penguin Books Ltd, Registered Offices: 80 Strand, London WC2R 0RL, England

Mad About Mad Libs ISBN 978-0-8431-7604-9

1 3 5 7 9 10 8 6 4 2

ALWAYS LEARNING   PEARSON

MAD LIBS®

UNDEAD
MAD LIBS

concept created by Roger Price and Leonard Stern

PSS!
PRICE STERN SLOAN
An Imprint of Penguin Group (USA) Inc.

INSTRUCTIONS

MAD LIBS® is a game for people who don't like games! It can be played by one, two, three, four, or forty.

● RIDICULOUSLY SIMPLE DIRECTIONS

In this tablet you will find stories containing blank spaces where words are left out. One player, the READER, selects one of these stories. The READER does not tell anyone what the story is about. Instead, he/she asks the other players, the WRITERS, to give him/her words. These words are used to fill in the blank spaces in the story.

● TO PLAY

The READER asks each WRITER in turn to call out a word—an adjective or a noun or whatever the space calls for—and uses them to fill in the blank spaces in the story. The result is a MAD LIBS game.

When the READER then reads the completed MAD LIBS® game to the other players, they will discover that they have written a story that is fantastic, screamingly funny, shocking, silly, crazy, or just plain dumb—depending upon which words each WRITER called out.

● EXAMPLE (Before and After)

"_____!" he said _____
         EXCLAMATION   ADVERB

as he jumped into his convertible _____ and
                               NOUN

drove off with his _____ wife.
                 ADJECTIVE

"*Ouch*!" he said *stupidly*
         EXCLAMATION   ADVERB

as he jumped into his convertible *cat* and
                               NOUN

drove off with his *brave* wife.
                 ADJECTIVE

QUICK REVIEW

In case you have forgotten what adjectives, adverbs, nouns, and verbs are, here is a quick review:

An **ADJECTIVE** describes something or somebody. *Lumpy, soft, ugly, messy,* and *short* are adjectives.

An **ADVERB** tells how something is done. It modifies a verb and usually ends in "ly." *Modestly, stupidly, greedily,* and *carefully* are adverbs.

A **NOUN** is the name of a person, place, or thing. *Sidewalk, umbrella, bridle, bathtub,* and *nose* are nouns.

A **VERB** is an action word. *Run, pitch, jump,* and *swim* are verbs. Put the verbs in past tense if the directions say PAST TENSE. *Ran, pitched, jumped,* and *swam* are verbs in the past tense.

When we ask for **A PLACE**, we mean any sort of place: a country or city *(Spain, Cleveland)* or a room *(bathroom, kitchen).*

An **EXCLAMATION** or **SILLY WORD** is any sort of funny sound, gasp, grunt, or outcry, like *Wow!, Ouch!, Whomp!, Ick!,* and *Gadzooks!*

When we ask for specific words, like a **NUMBER**, a **COLOR**, an **ANIMAL**, or a **PART OF THE BODY**, we mean a word that is one of those things, like *seven, blue, horse,* or *head.*

When we ask for a **PLURAL**, it means more than one. For example, *cat* pluralized is *cats.*

MAD LIBS® is fun to play with friends, but you can also play it by yourself! To begin with, DO NOT look at the story on the page below. Fill in the blanks on this page with the words called for. Then, using the words you have selected, fill in the blank spaces in the story.

Now you've created your own hilarious MAD LIBS® game!

CONFESSIONS OF A VAMPIRE'S GIRLFRIEND

PART OF THE BODY (PLURAL) _____

PERSON IN ROOM (MALE) _____

ADJECTIVE _____

NOUN _____

ADJECTIVE _____

ADJECTIVE _____

PLURAL NOUN _____

PART OF THE BODY _____

ADJECTIVE _____

PART OF THE BODY (PLURAL) _____

NOUN _____

NUMBER _____

ADJECTIVE _____

The moment I set my _____ on _____, I
    PART OF THE BODY (PLURAL)   PERSON IN ROOM (MALE)

knew we were meant to be. He was everything I wanted: tall, dark, and

_____. But love at first _____ isn't always
    ADJECTIVE   NOUN

picture-_____. The first time he gave me a/an
              ADJECTIVE

_____ rose, one of its _____ pricked my
    ADJECTIVE   PLURAL NOUN

_____ and drew blood. While I tried to find a bandage for
    PART OF THE BODY

the wound, he followed me to the bathroom—only to let loose a/an

_____ hiss, revealing his sharp _____.
    ADJECTIVE   PART OF THE BODY (PLURAL)

Luckily, he was able to restrain himself. But that's when I realized this hunky

_____ wasn't your average teenager. I had fallen in love with
    NOUN

a/an _____-year-old vampire, and I was _____
          NUMBER   ADJECTIVE

to be alive.

MAD LIBS® is fun to play with friends, but you can also play it by yourself! To begin with, DO NOT look at the story on the page below. Fill in the blanks on this page with the words called for. Then, using the words you have selected, fill in the blank spaces in the story.

Now you've created your own hilarious MAD LIBS® game!

IN THE DEAD OF NIGHT

ADJECTIVE _____

NOUN _____

PERSON IN ROOM (FEMALE) _____

ADJECTIVE _____

ADJECTIVE _____

ADJECTIVE _____

NOUN _____

ADJECTIVE _____

ADVERB _____

ADJECTIVE _____

PART OF THE BODY _____

ADJECTIVE _____

PART OF THE BODY (PLURAL) _____

MAD LIBS
IN THE DEAD OF NIGHT

It was a/an _____ and stormy _____.
ADJECTIVE   NOUN

_____ was alone in the woods, shivering in her
PERSON IN ROOM (FEMALE)

_____ dress, trying to find her way home. Suddenly she tripped
ADJECTIVE

over something _____ on the ground. She took a closer look
ADJECTIVE

and discovered it was a/an _____ tombstone! She was obviously
ADJECTIVE

in the middle of a/an _____-yard. Overcome by fear and
NOUN

struggling to stand up, she heard a/an _____ noise behind her.
ADJECTIVE

Someone or something was moving _____ toward her. She spun
ADVERB

around to get a better look and saw a/an _____ shadow moving
ADJECTIVE

past her. As the foggy figure came closer, she felt a cold _____
PART OF THE BODY

touch her arm. Shaking free, she ran out of the _____ cemetery
ADJECTIVE

as fast as her _____ could take her, never once
PART OF THE BODY (PLURAL)

looking back.

From UNDEAD MAD LIBS® · Copyright © 2011 by Price Stern Sloan,
an imprint of Penguin Group (USA) Inc., 345 Hudson Street, New York, NY 10014.

MAD LIBS® is fun to play with friends, but you can also play it by yourself! To begin with, DO NOT look at the story on the page below. Fill in the blanks on this page with the words called for. Then, using the words you have selected, fill in the blank spaces in the story.

Now you've created your own hilarious MAD LIBS® game!

INTERVIEW WITH A
CELEBRITY VAMPIRE

FIRST NAME _____

NOUN _____

PERSON IN ROOM (MALE) _____

ADJECTIVE _____

NOUN _____

NOUN _____

PERSON IN ROOM _____

ADJECTIVE _____

ADVERB _____

ADJECTIVE _____

CELEBRITY (MALE) _____

ADJECTIVE _____

ADJECTIVE _____

CELEBRITY (FEMALE) _____

NOUN _____

MAD LIBS
INTERVIEW WITH A
CELEBRITY VAMPIRE

Recently I, _____ Walters, sat down with _____-
FIRST NAME   NOUN

famous actor and vampire, _____, to discuss his most
PERSON IN ROOM (MALE)

recent work, his run-in with the law, and how he met his _____
ADJECTIVE

fiancée.

Q: How does it feel to have recently won the Motion Picture Academy

_____ for your performance in the coming-of-_____
NOUN   NOUN

movie, "The _____ Story"?
PERSON IN ROOM

A: It was a/an _____ honor just to be nominated.
ADJECTIVE

Q: Last month you were _____ arrested by the Hollywood
ADVERB

police for allegedly trying to turn someone into a/an _____
ADJECTIVE

vampire. Can you comment on that?

A: My friend _____ *wanted* to become a vampire. It was all a/an
CELEBRITY (MALE)

_____ misunderstanding.
ADJECTIVE

Q: Tell us about your romance with the _____ actress,
ADJECTIVE

_____.
CELEBRITY (FEMALE)

A: Let's just say I like to keep my private _____ private.
NOUN

A GRAVEYARD BASH

PERSON IN ROOM (MALE) _____

ADVERB _____

NOUN _____

ADJECTIVE _____

ADJECTIVE _____

VERB ENDING IN "ING" _____

NOUN _____

PLURAL NOUN _____

NOUN _____

ADJECTIVE _____

PERSON IN ROOM _____

SAME PERSON IN ROOM _____

MAD LIBS® is fun to play with friends, but you can also play it by yourself! To begin with, DO NOT look at the story on the page below. Fill in the blanks on this page with the words called for. Then, using the words you have selected, fill in the blank spaces in the story.

Now you've created your own hilarious MAD LIBS® game!

MAD LIBS®
A GRAVEYARD BASH

Dear _____ ,
           PERSON IN ROOM (MALE)

You are _____ invited to the most ghoulish _____
          ADVERB   NOUN

of the year!

Where: The _____ cemetery on Eternity Lane
                ADJECTIVE

When: Halloween night—at the _____ stroke of midnight
                                 ADJECTIVE

Why: If you're undead and enjoy _____ until the break of
                                       VERB ENDING IN "ING"

_____ , this shindig is for you! DJ Afterlife will be
        NOUN

spinning _____ all night, the Ghost of _____
            PLURAL NOUN   NOUN

Past will be bartending, and the devil himself may even make a/an

_____ guest appearance.
        ADJECTIVE

RSVP: Contact _____ the Zombie at _____-
               PERSON IN ROOM   SAME PERSON IN ROOM

zombie@zombiefriends.com.

From UNDEAD MAD LIBS® · Copyright © 2011 by Price Stern Sloan,
an imprint of Penguin Group (USA) Inc., 345 Hudson Street, New York, NY 10014.

MAD LIBS® is fun to play with friends, but you can also play it by yourself! To begin with, DO NOT look at the story on the page below. Fill in the blanks on this page with the words called for. Then, using the words you have selected, fill in the blank spaces in the story.

Now you've created your own hilarious MAD LIBS® game!

ARE YOU A VAMPIRE?

VERB _____

PART OF THE BODY _____

NOUN _____

ADJECTIVE _____

NOUN _____

NOUN _____

PLURAL NOUN _____

ADJECTIVE _____

ADVERB _____

ADJECTIVE _____

PLURAL NOUN _____

ADJECTIVE _____

MAD LIBS®
ARE YOU A VAMPIRE?

- Do you _____ with joy at the sight of blood?

VERB

- When you're hungry, does your _____ grow fangs?

PART OF THE BODY

- Do you sleep in a wooden _____ every day?

NOUN

- Do you avoid _____ sunlight for fear of turning into

ADJECTIVE

  a/an _____?

NOUN

- When you look into a/an _____, is your reflection missing?

NOUN

- Is biting _____ one of your _____

PLURAL NOUN   ADJECTIVE

  nighttime activities?

- Have you ever _____ turned one of your _____

ADVERB   ADJECTIVE

  friends into a vampire?

- Do you stay the same age no matter how many _____

PLURAL NOUN

  you've lived?

If you answered *yes* to any of these questions, you are probably

a/an _____ vampire.

ADJECTIVE

From UNDEAD MAD LIBS® · Copyright © 2011 by Price Stern Sloan,
an imprint of Penguin Group (USA) Inc., 345 Hudson Street, New York, NY 10014.

MAD LIBS is fun to play with friends, but you can also play it by yourself! To begin with, DO NOT look at the story on the page below. Fill in the blanks on this page with the words called for. Then, using the words you have selected, fill in the blank spaces in the story.

Now you've created your own hilarious MAD LIBS® game!

DAWN OF THE UNDEAD

_____ NOUN

_____ ADJECTIVE

_____ A PLACE

_____ PLURAL NOUN

_____ ADJECTIVE

_____ PLURAL NOUN

_____ ADJECTIVE

_____ ADJECTIVE

_____ NUMBER

_____ PLURAL NOUN

_____ ADJECTIVE

_____ PART OF THE BODY (PLURAL)

_____ VERB ENDING IN "ING"

_____ NOUN

_____ PLURAL NOUN

_____ ADJECTIVE

MAD LIBS
DAWN OF THE UNDEAD

We interrupt your regularly scheduled _____ to bring you
                                          NOUN

some _____ breaking news: A zombie outbreak in (the)
         ADJECTIVE

_____ is causing mass hysteria among the city's _____.
   A PLACE   PLURAL NOUN

The _____ zombie attack, believed to have started early this
        ADJECTIVE

morning, has claimed a growing number of _____. If you have
                                             PLURAL NOUN

any _____ information on the whereabouts of these
        ADJECTIVE

_____ creatures, call your local police at 9-1-_____.
   ADJECTIVE   NUMBER

Be on the lookout for anyone with yellow _____ and a/an
                                             PLURAL NOUN

_____ look in his or her _____. Please note
   ADJECTIVE   PART OF THE BODY (PLURAL)

that these creatures make _____ sounds and walk in a trancelike
                             VERB ENDING IN "ING"

_____ when looking for _____ to feed on.
   NOUN   PLURAL NOUN

Citizens are encouraged to stay indoors and remain calm, cool, and

_____.
   ADJECTIVE

MAD LIBS® is fun to play with friends, but you can also play it by yourself! To begin with, DO NOT look at the story on the page below. Fill in the blanks on this page with the words called for. Then, using the words you have selected, fill in the blank spaces in the story.

Now you've created your own hilarious MAD LIBS® game!

HOW TO PERFORM A SÉANCE

ADJECTIVE _____

NOUN _____

ADJECTIVE _____

ADJECTIVE _____

PLURAL NOUN _____

NOUN _____

ADJECTIVE _____

ADJECTIVE _____

PLURAL NOUN _____

PLURAL NOUN _____

PART OF THE BODY (PLURAL) _____

NOUN _____

ADVERB _____

ADJECTIVE _____

MAD LIBS®
HOW TO PERFORM A SÉANCE

Do you want a home, _____, home and not a haunted
                              ADJECTIVE

_____? Gather some _____ friends together
        NOUN   ADJECTIVE

late at night and have a/an _____ séance to get rid of any evil
                                   ADJECTIVE

spirits or ghostly _____ who just can't seem to cross over. First,
                        PLURAL NOUN

you'll need a wise _____ to preside over the gathering. He or
                          NOUN

she should have experience talking to _____ spirits. Second,
                                              ADJECTIVE

make sure to invite friends who feel really _____ about being
                                                   ADJECTIVE

there. No scaredy-_____ allowed. Once your friends arrive,
                      PLURAL NOUN

light some _____ to set the mood, sit next to one another, and
                PLURAL NOUN

hold _____. Then the medium should say, "Dear Spirit, if
        PART OF THE BODY (PLURAL)

you can hear us, tap three times on the _____." If all goes
                                               NOUN

_____, your _____ house will be ghost-free in
      ADVERB   ADJECTIVE

no time.

From UNDEAD MAD LIBS® · Copyright © 2011 by Price Stern Sloan,
an imprint of Penguin Group (USA) Inc., 345 Hudson Street, New York, NY 10014.

MAD LIBS® is fun to play with friends, but you can also play it by yourself! To begin with, DO NOT look at the story on the page below. Fill in the blanks on this page with the words called for. Then, using the words you have selected, fill in the blank spaces in the story.

Now you've created your own hilarious MAD LIBS® game!

DEMON DOS AND DON'TS

_____ ADJECTIVE

_____ PERSON IN ROOM

_____ ADJECTIVE

_____ PLURAL NOUN

_____ PART OF THE BODY

_____ PLURAL NOUN

_____ PERSON IN ROOM

_____ PLURAL NOUN

_____ NOUN

_____ PART OF THE BODY (PLURAL)

_____ ADJECTIVE

_____ PLURAL NOUN

MAD LIBS®
DEMON DOS AND DON'TS

When you come across a demon—the _____ spawn of
ADJECTIVE

_____—beware. These supernatural, super-_____
PERSON IN ROOM   ADJECTIVE

_____ are pure evil, so take heed of these dos and don'ts.
PLURAL NOUN

Do stay away from pitchfork-holding, fanged-_____ creatures.
PART OF THE BODY

Don't befriend, steal from, or give _____ to a demon.
PLURAL NOUN

Do be wary of anyone named Balthazar, Diablo, or Overlord _____.
PERSON IN ROOM

Don't accept any contracts from a demon promising millions of

_____ for signing your _____ away.
PLURAL NOUN   NOUN

Do check your friends' _____. Do they have red horns?
PART OF THE BODY (PLURAL)

If so, run! Those aren't your _____ friends, those are your
ADJECTIVE

worst _____!
PLURAL NOUN

A NIGHT AT THE
UNDEAD HOSPITAL

PERSON IN ROOM (FEMALE) _____

OCCUPATION _____

CELEBRITY _____

ADJECTIVE _____

NOUN _____

ADJECTIVE _____

ADJECTIVE _____

ADJECTIVE _____

PART OF THE BODY (PLURAL) _____

PLURAL NOUN _____

NOUN _____

ADJECTIVE _____

ADJECTIVE _____

PART OF THE BODY _____

LAST NAME _____

ADJECTIVE _____

NOUN _____

_____ just finished her first night as a/an
PERSON IN ROOM (FEMALE)

_____ at Saint _____ Hospital for the Undead. At
OCCUPATION   CELEBRITY

first, she was excited about her _____ job. She thought of it as a
                                  ADJECTIVE

charity _____, healing such _____ creatures as
         NOUN   ADJECTIVE

zombies and vampires when no one else would. But now she's not sure she'll

ever go back. The halls were dark and _____. Everywhere she
                                        ADJECTIVE

turned, she felt patients staring at her with a/an _____ look in
                                                    ADJECTIVE

their _____. She had to put casts on skeletons with
       PART OF THE BODY (PLURAL)

broken _____, give _____ injections to blood-
        PLURAL NOUN   NOUN

_____ vampires, and heal _____ zombies while they
ADJECTIVE   ADJECTIVE

foamed at the _____. Dr. _____ even asked her if
                PART OF THE BODY   LAST NAME

she'd like to become a vampire with him! The experience was truly

_____. And worst of all she now has two _____
ADJECTIVE   NOUN

marks on her neck that won't go away!

MAD LIBS® is fun to play with friends, but you can also play it by yourself! To begin with, DO NOT look at the story on the page below. Fill in the blanks on this page with the words called for. Then, using the words you have selected, fill in the blank spaces in the story.

Now you've created your own hilarious MAD LIBS® game!

BLENDING IN ON HALLOWEEN NIGHT

_____ NOUN

_____ ADVERB

_____ ADJECTIVE

_____ ADJECTIVE

_____ NOUN

_____ NOUN

_____ ADJECTIVE

_____ NOUN

_____ ADJECTIVE

_____ PLURAL NOUN

_____ NOUN

_____ ADJECTIVE

_____ ADJECTIVE

_____ NOUN

MAD LIBS®
BLENDING IN ON HALLOWEEN NIGHT

If you're a ghoul, a zombie, or a/an _____, Halloween is the
                                            NOUN

one night a year when you can walk among the living. In order to blend in

_____, follow these tried-and-_____ tips for passing
        ADVERB   ADJECTIVE

as a human.

• Be yourself! Who needs a costume when you're as _____
                                                          ADJECTIVE

as you are? Besides, no one wants to see a zombie dressed like Little Bo

_____ or Super-_____.
        NOUN   NOUN

• If someone offers you _____ candy, do not be
                                ADJECTIVE

alarmed. Act natural and say "Trick or _____!"
                                              NOUN

• Remember: You're trying to blend in. This means you can't bite

anyone. But you *can* scare people! What's Halloween without a few

_____ shrieks?
        ADJECTIVE

• Lastly, have fun! Go to human parties and bob for _____, carve
                                                        PLURAL NOUN

a/an _____, or enter a contest for the most _____
          NOUN   ADJECTIVE

costume. With your _____ looks, you just might win first
                          ADJECTIVE

_____!
    NOUN

MAD LIBS® is fun to play with friends, but you can also play it by yourself! To begin with, DO NOT look at the story on the page below. Fill in the blanks on this page with the words called for. Then, using the words you have selected, fill in the blank spaces in the story.

Now you've created your own hilarious MAD LIBS® game!

THE STORY OF
VAMPIRE CAT

ADJECTIVE _____

ADJECTIVE _____

ADJECTIVE _____

PART OF THE BODY _____

ADJECTIVE _____

ADJECTIVE _____

PERSON IN ROOM (MALE) _____

NOUN _____

ADVERB _____

ADJECTIVE _____

PLURAL NOUN _____

ADJECTIVE _____

NUMBER _____

SILLY WORD _____

VERB ENDING IN "ING" _____

PLURAL NOUN _____

ADJECTIVE _____

ADJECTIVE _____

MAD LIBS®
THE STORY OF VAMPIRE CAT

Once upon a time, a vampire was desperate for some _____
                                                      ADJECTIVE

blood. There were no humans around, and he was on the verge

of a/an _____ breakdown. He was searching everywhere for
        ADJECTIVE

victims when he spotted a/an _____ tabby cat that made his
                             ADJECTIVE

_____ water. He decided to make this _____
PART OF THE BODY   ADJECTIVE

little furball his student as well as his _____ victim. The cat,
                                          ADJECTIVE

renamed Count _____ VonCat, became the world's first feline
              PERSON IN ROOM (MALE)

vampire. Count VonCat terrorized the town of _____-ville and
                                             NOUN

used his _____ sweet purr and _____ stare to
         ADVERB   ADJECTIVE

lure innocent _____ into his clutches. To this day, Count
              PLURAL NOUN

VonCat continues his hunt—even at the ripe _____ age of
                                           ADJECTIVE

_____. He was last seen in the quiet village of _____,
NUMBER   SILLY WORD

_____ in alleyways and preying on _____ who
VERB ENDING IN "ING"   PLURAL NOUN

fall for his _____ cuteness and _____ charm.
             ADJECTIVE   ADJECTIVE

From UNDEAD MAD LIBS® · Copyright © 2011 by Price Stern Sloan,
an imprint of Penguin Group (USA) Inc., 345 Hudson Street, New York, NY 10014.

MAD LIBS® is fun to play with friends, but you can also play it by yourself! To begin with, DO NOT look at the story on the page below. Fill in the blanks on this page with the words called for. Then, using the words you have selected, fill in the blank spaces in the story.

Now you've created your own hilarious MAD LIBS® game!

THE CASE OF THE LIVING SKELETON

VERB ENDING IN "ING" _____

ADJECTIVE _____

ADJECTIVE _____

PLURAL NOUN _____

PERSON IN ROOM (MALE) _____

NOUN _____

ADJECTIVE _____

ADJECTIVE _____

NOUN _____

ADVERB _____

PART OF THE BODY _____

NOUN _____

ADJECTIVE _____

NOUN _____

It hasn't yet been proven, but I'm fairly certain that the skeleton in the

biology classroom is alive and _____. There's a rumor that the
                               VERB ENDING IN "ING"

_____ thing comes to life after school, performing
ADJECTIVE

_____ experiments on frogs and dissecting _____.
ADJECTIVE   PLURAL NOUN

And _____ swears that when he walked past the classroom
    PERSON IN ROOM (MALE)

after _____ practice, he saw the skeleton dancing. Finally, I
      NOUN

worked up the _____ courage to solve this _____
              ADJECTIVE   ADJECTIVE

mystery. One day, I hid underneath a/an _____ and waited for
                                        NOUN

the biology teacher to leave. Then I walked _____ toward the
                                            ADVERB

skeleton, tapped him on the shoulder, and bravely said, "Hello?" The

skeleton turned, slowly raising his right _____ to wave at me! I
                                          PART OF THE BODY

ran out of that room faster than a speeding _____. Now I have
                                            NOUN

a/an _____ excuse for never attending biology _____ again!
     ADJECTIVE   NOUN

HOW TO WARD
OFF A VAMPIRE

PLURAL NOUN _____

NOUN _____

ADJECTIVE _____

NOUN _____

ADJECTIVE _____

ADJECTIVE _____

ADJECTIVE _____

VERB _____

PLURAL NOUN _____

PLURAL NOUN _____

NOUN _____

PART OF THE BODY (PLURAL) _____

NOUN _____

NOUN _____

ADVERB _____

PART OF THE BODY _____

MAD LIBS® is fun to play with friends, but you can also play it by yourself! To begin with, DO NOT look at the story on the page below. Fill in the blanks on this page with the words called for. Then, using the words you have selected, fill in the blank spaces in the story.

Now you've created your own hilarious MAD LIBS® game!

MAD LIBS
HOW TO WARD OFF A VAMPIRE

All _____ beware. Fending off vampires takes more than common
         PLURAL NOUN

_____ and _____ intuition. Sure, you could carry
     NOUN   ADJECTIVE

around a sharp, wooden _____ to stop an attack, but you should
                              NOUN

also follow these four _____ suggestions:
                           ADJECTIVE

1. Vampires love the dark and hate the _____ sun, so run your
                                           ADJECTIVE

_____ errands in the daytime and don't _____ alone
   ADJECTIVE   VERB

in the middle of the night.

2. Vampires despise garlic and are allergic to holy _____, so carry
                                                      PLURAL NOUN

these _____ on your _____ at all times.
       PLURAL NOUN   NOUN

3. Vampires absolutely can't stand the sight of their hideous

_____ in a mirror. So always have a handheld
   PART OF THE BODY (PLURAL)

_____ in your pocket.
     NOUN

4. If you really want that pesky vampire to bite the dust and cross over to the

other _____, legend has it that there is only one way to
         NOUN

_____ stop a vampire: Cut off its _____.
   ADVERB   PART OF THE BODY

MAD LIBS® is fun to play with friends, but you can also play it by yourself! To begin with, DO NOT look at the story on the page below. Fill in the blanks on this page with the words called for. Then, using the words you have selected, fill in the blank spaces in the story.

Now you've created your own hilarious MAD LIBS® game!

FACTS ABOUT GHOULS

ADJECTIVE _____

ADVERB _____

NOUN _____

PLURAL NOUN _____

ADJECTIVE _____

ADJECTIVE _____

PLURAL NOUN _____

ADJECTIVE _____

PLURAL NOUN _____

PART OF THE BODY (PLURAL) _____

ADJECTIVE _____

ADJECTIVE _____

PLURAL NOUN _____

MAD LIBS®
FACTS ABOUT GHOULS

Of all the undead creatures, _____ ghouls are probably the most
ADJECTIVE

misunderstood. Contrary to popular belief, ghouls are _____
ADVERB

different from ghosts. They are undead monsters who live in

_____-yards and survive by gnawing on the _____
NOUN   PLURAL NOUN

found in _____ graves. The _____ appearance of these
ADJECTIVE   ADJECTIVE

evil _____ may shock you. Ghouls are extremely thin and
PLURAL NOUN

_____ with sharp teeth and _____, and their
ADJECTIVE   PLURAL NOUN

_____ are wrinkled and _____. Ghouls sleep
PART OF THE BODY (PLURAL)   ADJECTIVE

underground and emerge in packs at night—so next time you're wandering

in a/an _____ cemetery after dusk, be careful. These fiendish
ADJECTIVE

_____ might mistake you for dinner!
PLURAL NOUN

MAD LIBS® is fun to play with friends, but you can also play it by yourself! To begin with, DO NOT look at the story on the page below. Fill in the blanks on this page with the words called for. Then, using the words you have selected, fill in the blank spaces in the story.

Now you've created your own hilarious MAD LIBS® game!

A DIFFERENT KIND OF MOTHER

ADJECTIVE _____

PERSON IN ROOM (FEMALE) _____

ADJECTIVE _____

PLURAL NOUN _____

NOUN _____

PART OF THE BODY (PLURAL) _____

ADVERB _____

NOUN _____

ADJECTIVE _____

PART OF THE BODY _____

ADJECTIVE _____

PLURAL NOUN _____

PLURAL NOUN _____

LAST NAME _____

ADVERB _____

ADJECTIVE _____

PART OF THE BODY _____

NOUN _____

COLOR _____

Yesterday after school I went to my _____ friend

_____'s home to meet her _____ family. On
PERSON IN ROOM (FEMALE)   ADJECTIVE

the way there, she warned me about her mother: "My mom's not like other

_____. She's . . . different." "No big _____," I said,
PLURAL NOUN   NOUN

shrugging my _____. As we approached the house, the
PART OF THE BODY (PLURAL)

door swung open _____. One look and I jumped at least a/an
ADVERB

_____ high. My friend's mother was a/an _____
NOUN   ADJECTIVE

mummy, wrapped head to _____ in _____ strips of
PART OF THE BODY   ADJECTIVE

white _____! I was literally shaking in my _____. "Hi,
PLURAL NOUN   PLURAL NOUN

I'm Ms. _____, the mummy mommy. You're just in time," she
LAST NAME

said. "For what?" I asked _____. "Dinner! And I've got a/an
ADVERB

_____ surprise: We're having my famous _____
ADJECTIVE   PART OF THE BODY

lasagna." I didn't have to say a/an _____. I turned as
NOUN

_____ as a sheet and headed straight for home.
COLOR

MAD LIBS® is fun to play with friends, but you can also play it by yourself! To begin with, DO NOT look at the story on the page below. Fill in the blanks on this page with the words called for. Then, using the words you have selected, fill in the blank spaces in the story.

Now you've created your own hilarious MAD LIBS® game!

DRACULA

FIRST NAME _____

NOUN _____

ADJECTIVE _____

ADJECTIVE _____

NOUN _____

FIRST NAME (MALE) _____

PLURAL NOUN _____

PLURAL NOUN _____

PLURAL NOUN _____

VERB ENDING IN "ING" _____

CELEBRITY (FEMALE) _____

NOUN _____

ADJECTIVE _____

NOUN _____

ADVERB _____

MAD LIBS®
DRACULA

_____ Stoker's *Dracula* is a famous _____, written
    FIRST NAME   NOUN

in 1897, that tells the _____ story of Count Dracula, a vampire
                           ADJECTIVE

living in a/an _____ castle. The story begins with a young
                  ADJECTIVE

_____, _____ Harker, who visits the Count
      NOUN   FIRST NAME (MALE)

in order to discuss estate plans and other legal _____.
                                                        PLURAL NOUN

Harker quickly learns that Count Dracula is one of the most dangerous

_____ of all time. The Count puts Harker under a spell that
   PLURAL NOUN

makes him fall in love with three of Dracula's _____. Then the
                                                    PLURAL NOUN

blood-_____ Dracula takes a woman named _____
       VERB ENDING IN "ING"   CELEBRITY (FEMALE)

as his victim. Thankfully, by the book's end, Dracula is killed and turned

into _____ dust. The _____ Harker gets married
         NOUN   ADJECTIVE

to a beautiful _____ and lives _____ ever after.
                    NOUN   ADVERB

TEST YOUR UNDEAD IQ

ADJECTIVE _____

PLURAL NOUN _____

NOUN _____

ADJECTIVE _____

NOUN _____

PLURAL NOUN _____

NOUN _____

NOUN _____

NOUN _____

ADJECTIVE _____

NOUN _____

PERSON IN ROOM _____

NOUN _____

ADJECTIVE _____

ADJECTIVE _____

NOUN _____

ADJECTIVE _____

MAD LIBS® is fun to play with friends, but you can also play it by yourself! To begin with, DO NOT look at the story on the page below. Fill in the blanks on this page with the words called for. Then, using the words you have selected, fill in the blank spaces in the story.

Now you've created your own hilarious MAD LIBS® game!

MAD☺LIBS®
TEST YOUR UNDEAD IQ

Are you an undead expert? Take this _____ quiz to find out!
                                        ADJECTIVE

1. Where do vampires sleep? a) with the fishes, b) on the beach so they can

catch some _____, c) inside a/an _____, or d) in
              PLURAL NOUN   NOUN

a/an _____ coffin
       ADJECTIVE

2. What is a zombie's favorite snack? a) _____ salad, b) chocolate-
                                              NOUN

covered _____, c) _____ bits, or d) brains
         PLURAL NOUN   NOUN

3. Where do ghouls go to meet ghoul friends? a) the grocery _____,
                                                            NOUN

b) the _____ park, c) a/an _____ school, or
         NOUN   ADJECTIVE

d) the grave- _____
               NOUN

4. How do mummies become undead? a) they ask _____ nicely,
                                             PERSON IN ROOM

b) they travel through time using a/an _____ machine,
                                        NOUN

c) they earn extra _____ grades in school, or d) they get
                    ADJECTIVE

cursed by a/an _____ sorcerer
               ADJECTIVE

If you answered mostly Ds, you're a real undead _____! Your
                                                 NOUN

_____ expertise will come in handy—in this life and beyond . . .
 ADJECTIVE

MAD LIBS® is fun to play with friends, but you can also play it by yourself! To begin with, DO NOT look at the story on the page below. Fill in the blanks on this page with the words called for. Then, using the words you have selected, fill in the blank spaces in the story.

Now you've created your own hilarious MAD LIBS® game!

ANYTHING YOU VOODOO, I VOODOO BETTER

_____ PERSON IN ROOM (MALE)

_____ ADVERB

_____ NUMBER

_____ NOUN

_____ NOUN

_____ A PLACE

_____ NOUN

_____ VERB

_____ NOUN

_____ ADJECTIVE

_____ NOUN

_____ ADJECTIVE

_____ ADJECTIVE

_____ PLURAL NOUN

_____ ADJECTIVE

MAD LIBS®
ANYTHING YOU VOODOO,
I VOODOO BETTER

My name is Sorcerer _____, and I am a/an _____
PERSON IN ROOM (MALE)   ADVERB

trained voodoo master. In my years as a sorcerer, I have cursed more than

_____ dead people and turned them into _____-eating
NUMBER   NOUN

zombies. And now that they're under my _____ for eternity, I
NOUN

can take over (the) _____! Many will join me in my quest for
A PLACE

_____ domination. All I have to do is hold a séance, tell
NOUN

everyone to _____ into my crystal _____, think
VERB   NOUN

_____ thoughts, and stay very, very still. Then I use a special
ADJECTIVE

_____ to turn them into crusty, creepy, _____
NOUN   ADJECTIVE

zombies. From that point on, I can use mind control to make them attack

_____ cities and eat unsuspecting _____. I'm so
ADJECTIVE   PLURAL NOUN

powerful you might be under my _____ spell already . . .
ADJECTIVE

MAD LIBS® is fun to play with friends, but you can also play it by yourself! To begin with, DO NOT look at the story on the page below. Fill in the blanks on this page with the words called for. Then, using the words you have selected, fill in the blank spaces in the story.

Now you've created your own hilarious MAD LIBS® game!

FACTS ABOUT MUMMIES

_____ ADJECTIVE

_____ ADJECTIVE

_____ PLURAL NOUN

_____ PART OF THE BODY

_____ PLURAL NOUN

_____ PERSON IN ROOM (MALE)

_____ A PLACE

_____ PLURAL NOUN

_____ PART OF THE BODY

_____ A PLACE

_____ ADJECTIVE

_____ ADJECTIVE

_____ ADJECTIVE

_____ NOUN

_____ NOUN

MAD☺LIBS®
FACTS ABOUT MUMMIES

The history of the mummy goes all the way back to _____ Egypt,
                                                    ADJECTIVE

where mummification was a way of honoring the _____ dead.
                                               ADJECTIVE

Ancient Egyptians wrapped the bodies of important _____
                                                   PLURAL NOUN

from head to _____ to preserve them for eternity. Then they
              PART OF THE BODY

put them in a tomb along with their most important _____ to
                                                    PLURAL NOUN

carry them into the afterlife. Perhaps the most famous mummy is King

_____, who is currently on display at (the)
PERSON IN ROOM (MALE)

_____. But one of the oldest _____ ever found is
A PLACE   PLURAL NOUN

the Andean mummified _____, which is six thousand years old
                      PART OF THE BODY

and from (the) _____. While mummification is no longer in
                A PLACE

_____ fashion, some say that if a mummy's _____
ADJECTIVE   ADJECTIVE

tomb is disturbed, the _____ person inside will rise from the
                       ADJECTIVE

_____ and haunt the intruder for the rest of his or her
NOUN

_____.
NOUN

MAD LIBS® is fun to play with friends, but you can also play it by yourself! To begin with, DO NOT look at the story on the page below. Fill in the blanks on this page with the words called for. Then, using the words you have selected, fill in the blank spaces in the story.

Now you've created your own hilarious MAD LIBS® game!

UNDEAD CLASSIFIED ADS

ADJECTIVE _____

PLURAL NOUN _____

NOUN _____

ADJECTIVE _____

NOUN _____

NUMBER _____

ADJECTIVE _____

A PLACE _____

PERSON IN ROOM (MALE) _____

ADJECTIVE _____

ADJECTIVE _____

PLURAL NOUN _____

PART OF THE BODY _____

NOUN _____

ADJECTIVE _____

MAD LIBS
UNDEAD CLASSIFIED ADS

Are you a/an _____ vampire, zombie, mummy, or ghoul in
               ADJECTIVE

need of that special something? Look no further than the *New Undead Times*

classified ads, where you'll find all the _____ your evil heart desires.
                                          PLURAL NOUN

Skeleton Seeks Single, Bony _____: Male skeleton seeking a/an
                                    NOUN

_____, easygoing, and _____-loving lady skeleton
   ADJECTIVE   NOUN

to wine and dine. Must have all _____ bones intact. Those with
                                    NUMBER

_____ personalities preferred.
   ADJECTIVE

Coffin for Sale! Perfect condition. Used for only two centuries. Great for a

bedroom, basement, or (the) _____. Contact Count
                               A PLACE

_____ for details. _____ inquiries only.
PERSON IN ROOM (MALE)   ADJECTIVE

Zombie Puppies for Adoption: These _____, little creatures
                                          ADJECTIVE

might tear up your favorite pair of _____, foam at the
                                       PLURAL NOUN

_____, or try to turn you into a/an _____, but
PART OF THE BODY   NOUN

who cares! They're just too _____ to pass up.
                               ADJECTIVE

HOW TO SURVIVE
A ZOMBIE ATTACK

_____ NOUN

_____ NOUN

_____ ADJECTIVE

_____ ADJECTIVE

_____ PART OF THE BODY

_____ NOUN

_____ ADJECTIVE

_____ PLURAL NOUN

_____ NOUN

_____ ADJECTIVE

_____ NOUN

_____ ADJECTIVE

_____ PLURAL NOUN

_____ PLURAL NOUN

MAD LIBS® is fun to play with friends, but you can also play it by yourself! To begin with, DO NOT look at the story on the page below. Fill in the blanks on this page with the words called for. Then, using the words you have selected, fill in the blank spaces in the story.

Now you've created your own hilarious MAD LIBS® game!

Are zombies trying to take over your _____? Grab a/an
 NOUN

_____ immediately and start fending off those _____
 NOUN   ADJECTIVE

monsters before you become one yourself! Here are some _____
                                                         ADJECTIVE

tips for survival.

- Zombies want to eat your _____, so put on a/an
                              PART OF THE BODY

 _____ before heading out to save your _____ town.
  NOUN   ADJECTIVE

- You can become a zombie via a zombie bite. Therefore, wear a suit made

 of _____ to protect your skin. If you see that one of your friends
    PLURAL NOUN

 has a bite, stay far away. That friend may now be a/an _____!
                                                         NOUN

- Don't waste your _____ time trying to turn someone you
                    ADJECTIVE

 know back into a/an _____. There's no way to un-zombie
                       NOUN

 a/an _____ zombie.
        ADJECTIVE

- The phrase "Keep your friends close and your _____ closer"
                                                 PLURAL NOUN

 does not apply here! If you spot any zombies, run for the _____.
                                                            PLURAL NOUN

MAD LIBS®

HAPPILY EVER MAD LIBS

by Roger Price and Leonard Stern

PSS!

PRICE STERN SLOAN

An Imprint of Penguin Group (USA) Inc.

PRICE STERN SLOAN
Published by the Penguin Group
Penguin Group (USA) Inc., 375 Hudson Street, New York, New York 10014, USA
Penguin Group (Canada), 90 Eglinton Avenue East, Suite 700, Toronto, Ontario M4P 2Y3, Canada
(a division of Pearson Penguin Canada Inc.)
Penguin Books Ltd, 80 Strand, London WC2R 0RL, England
Penguin Ireland, 25 St Stephen's Green, Dublin 2, Ireland (a division of Penguin Books Ltd)
Penguin Group (Australia), 707 Collins Street, Melbourne, Victoria 3008, Australia
(a division of Pearson Australia Group Pty Ltd)
Penguin Books India Pvt Ltd, 11 Community Centre, Panchsheel Park, New Delhi—110 017, India
Penguin Group (NZ), 67 Apollo Drive, Rosedale, Auckland 0632, New Zealand
(a division of Pearson New Zealand Ltd)
Penguin Books (South Africa), Rosebank Office Park, 181 Jan Smuts Avenue,
Parktown North 2193, South Africa
Penguin China, B7 Jiaming Center, 27 East Third Ring Road North,
Chaoyang District, Beijing 100020, China

Penguin Books Ltd, Registered Offices: 80 Strand, London WC2R 0RL, England

Mad About Mad Libs published in 2013 by Price Stern Sloan,
a division of Penguin Young Readers Group, 345 Hudson Street, New York, New York 10014.

ALWAYS LEARNING   **PEARSON**

INSTRUCTIONS

MAD LIBS® is a game for people who don't like games!
It can be played by one, two, three, four, or forty.

• RIDICULOUSLY SIMPLE DIRECTIONS

In this tablet you will find stories containing blank spaces where words are left out. One player, the **READER**, selects one of these stories. The **READER** does not tell anyone what the story is about. Instead, he/she asks the other players, the **WRITERS**, to give him/her words. These words are used to fill in the blank spaces in the story.

• TO PLAY

The **READER** asks each **WRITER** in turn to call out a word—an adjective or a noun or whatever the space calls for—and uses them to fill in the blank spaces in the story. The result is a **MAD LIBS**® game.

When the **READER** then reads the completed **MAD LIBS**® game to the other players, they will discover that they have written a story that is fantastic, screamingly funny, shocking, silly, crazy, or just plain dumb—depending upon which words each **WRITER** called out.

• EXAMPLE (*Before* and *After*)

"_____!" he said _____
　　　　　EXCLAMATION　　　　　　　　　　　　　　　　ADVERB

as he jumped into his convertible _____ and
　　　　　　　　　　　　　　　　　　　　　　　　NOUN

drove off with his _____ wife.
　　　　　　　　　　　　ADJECTIVE

"_____*Ouch*_____!" he said _____*stupidly*_____
　　　EXCLAMATION　　　　　　　　　　　ADVERB

as he jumped into his convertible _____*cat*_____ and
　　　　　　　　　　　　　　　　　　　　NOUN

drove off with his _____*brave*_____ wife.
　　　　　　　　　　ADJECTIVE

MAD LIBS®

QUICK REVIEW

In case you have forgotten what adjectives, adverbs, nouns, and verbs are, here is a quick review:

An **ADJECTIVE** describes something or somebody. *Lumpy, soft, ugly, messy,* and *short* are adjectives.

An **ADVERB** tells how something is done. It modifies a verb and usually ends in "ly." *Modestly, stupidly, greedily,* and *carefully* are adverbs.

A **NOUN** is the name of a person, place, or thing. *Sidewalk, umbrella, bridle, bathtub,* and *nose* are nouns.

A **VERB** is an action word. *Run, pitch, jump,* and *swim* are verbs. Put the verbs in past tense if the directions say PAST TENSE. *Ran, pitched, jumped,* and *swam* are verbs in the past tense.

When we ask for **A PLACE**, we mean any sort of place: a country or city (*Spain, Cleveland*) or a room (*bathroom, kitchen*).

An **EXCLAMATION** or **SILLY WORD** is any sort of funny sound, gasp, grunt, or outcry, like *Wow!, Ouch!, Whomp!, Ick!,* and *Gadzooks!*

When we ask for specific words, like a **NUMBER**, a **COLOR**, an **ANIMAL**, or a **PART OF THE BODY**, we mean a word that is one of those things, like *seven, blue, horse,* or *head.*

When we ask for a **PLURAL**, it means more than one. For example, *cat* pluralized is *cats.*

JACK AND THE BEANSTALK

_____	NOUN
_____	NOUN
_____	PERSON IN ROOM
_____	PLURAL NOUN
_____	ADJECTIVE
_____	NOUN
_____	PART OF THE BODY (PLURAL)
_____	ADJECTIVE
_____	ADJECTIVE
_____	SILLY WORD
_____	PLURAL NOUN
_____	NUMBER

MAD LIBS
JACK AND THE BEANSTALK

Once upon a time, there was a/an _____ named Jack who lived

NOUN

with his mother in a tiny _____. The only thing they owned was

NOUN

a cow named _____. Jack's mom told him to sell the cow to buy

PERSON IN ROOM

some _____. On his way to the market, Jack met a stranger who

PLURAL NOUN

said, "I'll trade you these _____ beans for your cow." Jack agreed,

ADJECTIVE

but when his mom learned he had disobeyed her, she was angrier than a wild

_____ and threw the beans out the window. As they slept, the

NOUN

beans grew into a gigantic beanstalk. When Jack awoke, he couldn't believe

his _____. He immediately climbed the _____

PART OF THE BODY (PLURAL) ADJECTIVE

beanstalk. At the top, he met a/an _____ giant. "Fee, fi, fo,

ADJECTIVE

_____ !" the angry giant bellowed. Jack quickly escaped,

SILLY WORD

grabbing a hen that laid golden _____ , and quickly climbed

PLURAL NOUN

down the beanstalk. With their newfound wealth, Jack and his mother

bought _____ cows and lived happily ever after.

NUMBER

From HAPPILY EVER MAD LIBS® · Copyright © 2010 by Price Stern Sloan,
an imprint of Penguin Group (USA) Inc., 345 Hudson Street, New York, NY 10014.

MAD LIBS® is fun to play with friends, but you can also play it by yourself! To begin with, DO NOT look at the story on the page below. Fill in the blanks on this page with the words called for. Then, using the words you have selected, fill in the blank spaces in the story.

Now you've created your own hilarious MAD LIBS® game!

LIVE WITH HANSEL AND GRETEL

ADJECTIVE _____

PLURAL NOUN _____

ADJECTIVE _____

ADJECTIVE _____

PLURAL NOUN _____

PLURAL NOUN _____

ADJECTIVE _____

NOUN _____

PLURAL NOUN _____

NOUN _____

ADJECTIVE _____

CELEBRITY _____

MAD LIBS®
LIVE WITH HANSEL AND GRETEL

The following is a/an _____ interview to be read aloud by three
_____ADJECTIVE_____

_____:
___PLURAL NOUN___

Host: Welcome to *Fairy Tale Forum*. We're here live with the _____
_____ADJECTIVE

Hansel and Gretel. Gretel, tell us what happened.

Gretel: Well, our _____ stepmother kept taking us into the
_____ADJECTIVE_____

woods so we'd get lost.

Hansel: But I left a trail of _____ so we could find our way back.
_____PLURAL NOUN

Host: But then something unexpected happened, right?

Gretel: Yes. We found a house made entirely of candy _____.
_____PLURAL NOUN

Hansel: And we were so _____ that we started to eat it. But
_____ADJECTIVE

then a witch popped out and put me in a/an _____.
_____NOUN

Host: Oh, my _____! How did you escape?
_____PLURAL NOUN

Hansel: Gretel pushed the witch into a/an _____ and
_____NOUN

we ran home.

Host: What a/an _____ story. Viewers, join us next time when
_____ADJECTIVE

we find out if Prince Charming is secretly dating _____.
_____CELEBRITY

MAD LIBS® is fun to play with friends, but you can also play it by yourself! To begin with, DO NOT look at the story on the page below. Fill in the blanks on this page with the words called for. Then, using the words you have selected, fill in the blank spaces in the story.

Now you've created your own hilarious MAD LIBS® game!

THE WOLF'S SIDE
OF THE STORY

_____ ADJECTIVE

_____ VERB ENDING IN "ING"

_____ ADJECTIVE

_____ NOUN

_____ PART OF THE BODY (PLURAL)

_____ PLURAL NOUN

_____ NOUN

_____ NOUN

_____ PLURAL NOUN

_____ PART OF THE BODY (PLURAL)

_____ ADJECTIVE

_____ NOUN

_____ ADJECTIVE

_____ ADJECTIVE

I am the big, _____ wolf. You may have heard the lies Little Red
       ADJECTIVE

_____ Hood has told about me. But now it's my turn to
VERB ENDING IN "ING"

tell you the truth. One day Little Red Riding Hood was on her way to visit

her _____ grandmother. But I happened to get there first. I
    ADJECTIVE

knocked, but there was no answer. Then I remembered it was Wednesday

and Grandma would be at her weekly _____ game. I'd been on
         NOUN

my _____ all day, so I decided to let myself in to take a
    PART OF THE BODY (PLURAL)

nap. It was freezing in the house, so I slipped into one of Grandma's

_____ and fell into a deep _____ . I was awakened
   PLURAL NOUN   NOUN

by Little Red Riding _____ shouting at me, saying insulting
       NOUN

things like, "What big _____ you have!" and "What big
       PLURAL NOUN

_____ you have." Offended, I got up and left. Believe
PART OF THE BODY (PLURAL)

me, that's the _____ truth and nothing but the _____ .
     ADJECTIVE   NOUN

So, you see, I'm not the _____ fiend Little Red makes me out to
       ADJECTIVE

be. I'm the real victim in this _____ tale!
         ADJECTIVE

MAD LIBS® is fun to play with friends, but you can also play it by yourself! To begin with, DO NOT look at the story on the page below. Fill in the blanks on this page with the words called for. Then, using the words you have selected, fill in the blank spaces in the story.

Now you've created your own hilarious MAD LIBS® game!

CASTLE FOR SALE

OCCUPATION _____

ADJECTIVE _____

ADJECTIVE _____

PERSON IN ROOM (MALE) _____

ADJECTIVE _____

ADJECTIVE _____

A PLACE _____

ADJECTIVE _____

PART OF THE BODY _____

PART OF THE BODY _____

PLURAL NOUN _____

NOUN _____

ADVERB _____

NOUN _____

VERB _____

ADJECTIVE _____

PLURAL NOUN _____

PLURAL NOUN _____

ADJECTIVE _____

NUMBER _____

MAD LIBS®
CASTLE FOR SALE

Are you a king, queen, or _____ looking for that perfectly
<u>OCCUPATION</u>

_____ new home? Then have we got a/an _____ place
<u>ADJECTIVE</u>   <u>ADJECTIVE</u>

for you! King _____'s _____ castle has just come
<u>PERSON IN ROOM (MALE)</u>   <u>ADJECTIVE</u>

on the market! Originally built in the _____ Ages, this lakefront
<u>ADJECTIVE</u>

wonder has towers that rise high above (the) _____ and a/an
<u>A PLACE</u>

_____ view that will take your _____ away. In each
<u>ADJECTIVE</u>   <u>PART OF THE BODY</u>

and every room of this 25,000 square-_____ masterpiece, there
<u>PART OF THE BODY</u>

are magnificent stained glass _____ and splendid Gothic
<u>PLURAL NOUN</u>

_____-burning fireplaces. There's also a chef's state-of-the-art,
<u>NOUN</u>

_____ modern _____ for those who love to
<u>ADVERB</u>   <u>NOUN</u>

_____. For security and _____ privacy, there is also a
<u>VERB</u>   <u>ADJECTIVE</u>

moat filled with _____ and a drawbridge to keep out unwanted
<u>PLURAL NOUN</u>

_____. Take advantage of the collapse in the castle market and
<u>PLURAL NOUN</u>

make a/an _____ offer on this treasure. The asking price is a
<u>ADJECTIVE</u>

ridiculously low _____ dollars.
<u>NUMBER</u>

MAD LIBS® is fun to play with friends, but you can also play it by yourself! To begin with, DO NOT look at the story on the page below. Fill in the blanks on this page with the words called for. Then, using the words you have selected, fill in the blank spaces in the story.

Now you've created your own hilarious MAD LIBS® game!

CINDERELLA

ADJECTIVE _____

ADJECTIVE _____

ADJECTIVE _____

PART OF THE BODY _____

NOUN _____

ADJECTIVE _____

NOUN _____

NOUN _____

NOUN _____

NOUN _____

PLURAL NOUN _____

PERSON IN ROOM (MALE) _____

PLURAL NOUN _____

PART OF THE BODY _____

ADVERB _____

MAD LIBS
CINDERELLA

There once was a/an _____ young girl named Cinderella who
ADJECTIVE

lived with her _____ stepmother and two _____
ADJECTIVE   ADJECTIVE

stepsisters. She waited on them hand and _____, but they treated
PART OF THE BODY

her like a/an _____. Cinderella heard about a ball the prince was
NOUN

throwing, but she didn't have a/an _____ gown to wear. Then,
ADJECTIVE

out of the clear, blue _____, her fairy _____-mother
NOUN   NOUN

appeared and waved her magic _____. Cinderella's ragged clothes
NOUN

turned into a beautiful _____, and her worn work shoes became a pair
NOUN

of glass _____. Cinderella went to the ball and danced with Prince
PLURAL NOUN

_____, who fell madly in love with her. But at the stroke of
PERSON IN ROOM (MALE)

midnight she had to flee, losing one of her glass _____. The prince
PLURAL NOUN

traveled throughout the kingdom, trying the slipper on the _____
PART OF THE BODY

of every young girl, but, of course, it fit only one—Cinderella! The two were

soon married and lived _____ ever after.
ADVERB

From HAPPILY EVER MAD LIBS® · Copyright © 2010 by Price Stern Sloan,
an imprint of Penguin Group (USA) Inc., 345 Hudson Street, New York, NY 10014.

MAD LIBS® is fun to play with friends, but you can also play it by yourself! To begin with, DO NOT look at the story on the page below. Fill in the blanks on this page with the words called for. Then, using the words you have selected, fill in the blank spaces in the story.

Now you've created your own hilarious MAD LIBS® game!

PRINCESS SEEKING FAIRY GODMOTHER

ADJECTIVE _____

PERSON IN ROOM (FEMALE) _____

ADJECTIVE _____

ADJECTIVE _____

NUMBER _____

ADJECTIVE _____

PLURAL NOUN _____

NOUN _____

PLURAL NOUN _____

PLURAL NOUN _____

PLURAL NOUN _____

PLURAL NOUN _____

VERB ENDING IN "ING" _____

ADJECTIVE _____

PLURAL NOUN _____

PLURAL NOUN _____

PART OF THE BODY (PLURAL) _____

ADVERB _____

MAD LIBS®
PRINCESS SEEKING
FAIRY GODMOTHER

Wanted: One _____ godmother needed immediately for
ADJECTIVE

_____ , a very _____ young princess
PERSON IN ROOM (FEMALE)   ADJECTIVE

with a/an _____ personality. Applicant must have at least
ADJECTIVE

_____ years of _____ experience helping princesses
NUMBER   ADJECTIVE

or other royal _____ live up to their _____ and
PLURAL NOUN   NOUN

making their _____ come true. The ideal candidate should be
PLURAL NOUN

able to turn pumpkins into _____ and mice into _____
PLURAL NOUN   PLURAL NOUN

who are capable of pulling oversized _____ . Since the princess
PLURAL NOUN

enjoys ballroom _____ with _____ princes,
VERB ENDING IN "ING"   ADJECTIVE

expertise in waltzes, polkas, and _____ is a must. Salary will be
PLURAL NOUN

paid in golden _____—as many as you can carry in your
PLURAL NOUN

_____ . Please apply as _____ as possible!
PART OF THE BODY (PLURAL)   ADVERB

FROM A SPELL BOOK
FOR WICKED QUEENS

ADJECTIVE _____

ADJECTIVE _____

ADJECTIVE _____

ADJECTIVE _____

NOUN _____

NOUN _____

PART OF THE BODY _____

ADJECTIVE _____

NUMBER _____

PART OF THE BODY _____

NUMBER _____

NOUN _____

TYPE OF LIQUID _____

ADJECTIVE _____

ADJECTIVE _____

ADJECTIVE _____

ADJECTIVE _____

MAD LIBS® is fun to play with friends, but you can also play it by yourself! To begin with, DO NOT look at the story on the page below. Fill in the blanks on this page with the words called for. Then, using the words you have selected, fill in the blank spaces in the story.

Now you've created your own hilarious MAD LIBS® game!

MAD LIBS®
FROM A SPELL BOOK
FOR WICKED QUEENS

Need to make a/an _____ princess fall into a deep,
ADJECTIVE

_____ sleep? Here is a recipe that will bring incredibly
ADJECTIVE

_____ results. First, put a large _____
ADJECTIVE   ADJECTIVE

cauldron, filled to the brim with _____ , on an open
TYPE OF LIQUID

_____ and heat to _____ degrees. When it begins
NOUN   NUMBER

to boil, add a/an _____ from a newt and _____
PART OF THE BODY   NUMBER

freshly caught _____ lizards. Mash them up well and mix
ADJECTIVE

with the _____ of a toad and the _____ of a
PART OF THE BODY   NOUN

small, furry _____ . Once again, bring to a/an _____
NOUN   ADJECTIVE

boil. Now you can offer the brew to any unsuspecting _____
ADJECTIVE

princess. They fall for it every time. But beware: No matter how strong the

_____ potion is, true love will reverse its _____
ADJECTIVE   ADJECTIVE

spell every time!

MAD LIBS® is fun to play with friends, but you can also play it by yourself! To begin with, DO NOT look at the story on the page below. Fill in the blanks on this page with the words called for. Then, using the words you have selected, fill in the blank spaces in the story.

Now you've created your own hilarious MAD LIBS® game!

THE THREE
BILLY GOATS GRUFF

ADJECTIVE _____

ADJECTIVE _____

ADJECTIVE _____

NOUN _____

VERB _____

NOUN _____

NOUN _____

ADJECTIVE _____

NOUN _____

ADVERB _____

EXCLAMATION _____

NOUN _____

NOUN _____

MAD LIBS®
THE THREE
BILLY GOATS GRUFF

Once there were three _____ billy goats with the last name of

ADJECTIVE

Gruff. They wanted to cross a river to eat the _____ grass on

ADJECTIVE

the other side. But the bridge was guarded by a fearsome, _____

ADJECTIVE

troll who devoured any _____ who tried to cross it. When the

NOUN

first and littlest billy goat started to _____ over the bridge,

VERB

the terrifying _____ shouted, "I'm going to eat you!"

NOUN

Thinking fast on his _____ , the billy goat said, "Wait, I have

NOUN

a brother who is bigger and more _____ than I am. You can

ADJECTIVE

eat him." So the troll waited for the next billy _____ . When

NOUN

he appeared, the same thing happened. So the troll waited _____

ADVERB

for the third and biggest billy goat. This time the troll jumped out and cried,

"_____ ! I am going to eat you!" But the biggest billy goat

EXCLAMATION

simply lifted the troll with his horns and knocked him into the raging

_____ below. From then on, the billy goats feasted in the

NOUN

fields on the other side of the _____ to their hearts' content.

NOUN

MAD LIBS® is fun to play with friends, but you can also play it by yourself! To begin with, DO NOT look at the story on the page below. Fill in the blanks on this page with the words called for. Then, using the words you have selected, fill in the blank spaces in the story.

Now you've created your own hilarious MAD LIBS® game!

RECIPE FOR THE BEST PORRIDGE EVER

PERSON IN ROOM (FEMALE) _____

PLURAL NOUN _____

ADJECTIVE _____

NOUN _____

ADJECTIVE _____

ADJECTIVE _____

PLURAL NOUN _____

ADJECTIVE _____

PLURAL NOUN _____

NUMBER _____

NOUN _____

ADJECTIVE _____

PLURAL NOUN _____

ADJECTIVE _____

ADJECTIVE _____

NOUN _____

PLURAL NOUN _____

MAD LIBS®
RECIPE FOR THE
BEST PORRIDGE EVER

Hi. I'm _____ , but you probably know me as Mama Bear
PERSON IN ROOM (FEMALE)

from *Goldilocks and the Three* _____ . I'm here to tell you
PLURAL NOUN

about making incredibly _____ porridge. Lots of folks
ADJECTIVE

say that eating my porridge is even better than eating a juicy sirloin

_____ . To make really _____ porridge, you
NOUN   ADJECTIVE

start by filling a/an _____ pot with water. Then add two cups
ADJECTIVE

of oats, a few chopped _____ , and plenty of _____
PLURAL NOUN   ADJECTIVE

_____ . Place the pot on the stove for _____ hours.
PLURAL NOUN   NUMBER

Stir with a/an _____ so it will be nice and _____ . This
NOUN   ADJECTIVE

recipe should amply serve three bears or fifty-three _____ . Now,
PLURAL NOUN

some like it _____ , some like it _____ , and some
ADJECTIVE   ADJECTIVE

like it just right. And, by the way, unless you plan to share this porridge, be

on the lookout for _____ -stealing girls named Goldi- _____ .
NOUN   PLURAL NOUN

MAD LIBS® is fun to play with friends, but you can also play it by yourself! To begin with, DO NOT look at the story on the page below. Fill in the blanks on this page with the words called for. Then, using the words you have selected, fill in the blank spaces in the story.

Now you've created your own hilarious MAD LIBS® game!

RUMPELSTILTSKIN

OCCUPATION _____

ADJECTIVE _____

NOUN _____

ADJECTIVE _____

PART OF THE BODY _____

PLURAL NOUN _____

NOUN _____

NOUN _____

ADVERB _____

ADJECTIVE _____

PART OF THE BODY (PLURAL) _____

ADJECTIVE _____

MAD LIBS®
RUMPELSTILTSKIN

There once was a greedy _____ who said that his daughter
OCCUPATION

could spin straw into gold. The _____ king put the girl in a
ADJECTIVE

room filled with straw and gave her until the _____ rose to prove
NOUN

herself. She knew she wasn't capable of such a feat, but at midnight, a/an

_____ man appeared. "I'll turn the straw into gold if you give
ADJECTIVE

me the necklace around your _____," he said. She did,
PART OF THE BODY

and the room filled with golden _____. The same thing
PLURAL NOUN

happened the next night and cost the girl her _____. On the
NOUN

third night, she had nothing to offer. "In that case," he said, "your firstborn

_____ will be mine." She _____ agreed. But when
NOUN   ADVERB

the girl was happily married to the king and they had a baby, the little man

reappeared. He said, "If you can guess my name, I will release you from your

_____ promise." "Rumpelstiltskin," the queen guessed. The
ADJECTIVE

little man couldn't believe his _____. She was right! So
PART OF THE BODY (PLURAL)

Rumpelstiltskin raced out of the castle in a/an _____ rage.
ADJECTIVE

From HAPPILY EVER MAD LIBS® · Copyright © 2010 by Price Stern Sloan,
an imprint of Penguin Group (USA) Inc., 345 Hudson Street, New York, NY 10014.

MAD LIBS® is fun to play with friends, but you can also play it by yourself! To begin with, DO NOT look at the story on the page below. Fill in the blanks on this page with the words called for. Then, using the words you have selected, fill in the blank spaces in the story.

Now you've created your own hilarious MAD LIBS® game!

HOW TO BE A PRINCESS

PART OF THE BODY _____

ADJECTIVE _____

ADJECTIVE _____

PLURAL NOUN _____

ADJECTIVE _____

ADJECTIVE _____

NOUN _____

ADVERB _____

ADJECTIVE _____

ADJECTIVE _____

ADJECTIVE _____

VERB ENDING IN "ING" _____

ADJECTIVE _____

ADJECTIVE _____

ADVERB _____

MAD LIBS
HOW TO BE A PRINCESS

It is difficult not to envy a young woman who has everything her

_____ desires. But history shows it isn't easy being a princess.
PART OF THE BODY

You have to maintain _____ standards and abide by
ADJECTIVE

_____ rules. For example:
ADJECTIVE

• A princess should always be kind to, and understanding of, her royal

_____ . A princess knows that a/an _____
PLURAL NOUN   ADJECTIVE

smile is preferable to a/an _____ frown.
ADJECTIVE

• A princess should be a patron of the arts, well-versed in classical

_____ , and _____ familiar with _____
NOUN   ADVERB   ADJECTIVE

authors and their _____ works.
ADJECTIVE

• A princess should never make a/an _____ decision. She
ADJECTIVE

should always think before _____ . And when she does
VERB ENDING IN "ING"

speak, she should be articulate and, if possible, very _____.
ADJECTIVE

• And, of course, a princess must be prepared to marry a/an _____
ADJECTIVE

prince and live _____ ever after.
ADVERB

From HAPPILY EVER MAD LIBS® · Copyright © 2010 by Price Stern Sloan,
an imprint of Penguin Group (USA) Inc., 345 Hudson Street, New York, NY 10014.

MAD LIBS® is fun to play with friends, but you can also play it by yourself! To begin with, DO NOT look at the story on the page below. Fill in the blanks on this page with the words called for. Then, using the words you have selected, fill in the blank spaces in the story.

Now you've created your own hilarious MAD LIBS® game!

MAGICAL WEDDING INVITATION

_____ PERSON IN ROOM (FEMALE)

_____ PERSON IN ROOM (MALE)

_____ ADJECTIVE

_____ ADJECTIVE

_____ CELEBRITY (FEMALE)

_____ PLURAL NOUN

_____ CELEBRITY (MALE)

_____ A PLACE

_____ ADJECTIVE

_____ ARTICLE OF CLOTHING (PLURAL)

_____ NOUN

_____ PLURAL NOUN

_____ ADJECTIVE

_____ PERSON IN ROOM

_____ PLURAL NOUN

_____ ADJECTIVE

MAD LIBS
MAGICAL WEDDING
INVITATION

You are hereby cordially invited by Queen _____ and
                                              PERSON IN ROOM (FEMALE)

King _____ to a most _____ event—the marriage
      PERSON IN ROOM (MALE)   ADJECTIVE

of Sleeping Beauty to the most _____ Prince Charming. The
                                    ADJECTIVE

bride will be attended by her maid of honor, _____ , and her
                                                CELEBRITY (FEMALE)

seven _____ , while _____ is the best
           PLURAL NOUN   CELEBRITY (MALE)

man. The ceremony will take place in the enchanted forest near (the)

_____ . All female guests are encouraged to wear _____
   A PLACE   ADJECTIVE

dresses, while for men, fancy _____ are recommended.
                                ARTICLE OF CLOTHING (PLURAL)

The dinner menu will include roast _____ and sweet
                                        NOUN

_____ for dessert. The band, _____
   PLURAL NOUN   ADJECTIVE

_____ and the _____ , will provide music for
PERSON IN ROOM   PLURAL NOUN

dancing. Please RSVP at your earliest convenience. A/An _____
                                                           ADJECTIVE

time is guaranteed for all.

From HAPPILY EVER MAD LIBS® · Copyright © 2010 by Price Stern Sloan,
an imprint of Penguin Group (USA) Inc., 345 Hudson Street, New York, NY 10014.

MAD LIBS® is fun to play with friends, but you can also play it by yourself! To begin with, DO NOT look at the story on the page below. Fill in the blanks on this page with the words called for. Then, using the words you have selected, fill in the blank spaces in the story.

Now you've created your own hilarious MAD LIBS® game!

SNOW WHITE AT THE SEVEN DWARFS' COTTAGE

_____ ADJECTIVE

_____ PERSON IN ROOM (FEMALE)

_____ A PLACE

_____ ADJECTIVE

_____ PLURAL NOUN

_____ PLURAL NOUN

_____ ADJECTIVE

_____ PLURAL NOUN

_____ PLURAL NOUN

_____ NOUN

_____ PERSON IN ROOM

_____ PERSON IN ROOM

_____ ADJECTIVE

_____ ADJECTIVE

_____ A PLACE

_____ OCCUPATION

My name is Snow White, and I am hiding from my _____
                                                ADJECTIVE

stepmother, _____, at the Seven Dwarfs' cottage in (the)
            PERSON IN ROOM (FEMALE)

_____. It is a/an _____ little place with a roof
  A PLACE   ADJECTIVE

made of _____. Since the dwarfs are letting me stay here, I
         PLURAL NOUN

help out by dusting the _____, cooking _____
                         PLURAL NOUN   ADJECTIVE

dinners, and washing their _____. The dwarfs and I have become
                            PLURAL NOUN

really close _____ and enjoy one another's _____
              PLURAL NOUN   NOUN

very much. Their names are Sleepy, Happy, _____,
                                            PERSON IN ROOM

_____, Sneezy, _____, and Doc. The dwarfs
  PERSON IN ROOM   ADJECTIVE

and I share many _____ interests. We especially like to sing,
                  ADJECTIVE

"Hi ho, hi ho, it's off to (the) _____ we go!" Oh, sorry, have
                                  A PLACE

to run now. There's a sweet, old _____ at the door selling apples.
                                  OCCUPATION

MAD LIBS® is fun to play with friends, but you can also play it by yourself! To begin with, DO NOT look at the story on the page below. Fill in the blanks on this page with the words called for. Then, using the words you have selected, fill in the blank spaces in the story.

Now you've created your own hilarious MAD LIBS® game!

THE GINGERBREAD MAN'S
EXERCISE ROUTINE

VERB _____

SAME VERB _____

NOUN _____

ADJECTIVE _____

PLURAL NOUN _____

ADJECTIVE _____

ADVERB _____

ADJECTIVE _____

NOUN _____

PART OF THE BODY (PLURAL) _____

NUMBER _____

NOUN _____

PART OF THE BODY _____

VERB _____

PART OF THE BODY _____

NOUN _____

ADJECTIVE _____

NOUN _____

PLURAL NOUN _____

MAD LIBS
THE GINGERBREAD MAN'S EXERCISE ROUTINE

_____ , _____ as fast as you can. You can't
     VERB   SAME VERB

catch me—I'm the Gingerbread _____ ! And I'm known for
                      NOUN

running at _____ speeds to keep people and _____
         ADJECTIVE   PLURAL NOUN

from trying to eat me. I guess it's because I smell so _____ .
                                    ADJECTIVE

But I have to work _____ hard to stay in _____
               ADVERB   ADJECTIVE

shape. I start my day when the _____ comes up. I warm up by
                         NOUN

stretching to loosen my _____ for approximately
                   PART OF THE BODY (PLURAL)

_____ minutes. For weight lifting exercises, I lift a candy
     NUMBER

_____ over my head to strengthen my abs and
     NOUN

_____ . I do _____-ups to develop strength in
 PART OF THE BODY   VERB

my _____ . And I always eat a healthy breakfast that includes
    PART OF THE BODY

lots of shredded _____ . This routine may sound a little
               NOUN

_____ , but it can really make you feel as fit as a/an
    ADJECTIVE

_____ . And you'll never have to worry about getting eaten by
     NOUN

hungry _____ !
      PLURAL NOUN

UNDER THE SEA WITH THE LITTLE MERMAID

_____ PLURAL NOUN

_____ ADJECTIVE

_____ ADJECTIVE

_____ PLURAL NOUN

_____ PERSON IN ROOM (MALE)

_____ NOUN

_____ PLURAL NOUN

_____ NOUN

_____ PLURAL NOUN

_____ VERB

_____ PART OF THE BODY (PLURAL)

_____ VERB

_____ PLURAL NOUN

_____ ADJECTIVE

_____ PLURAL NOUN

_____ PART OF THE BODY (PLURAL)

_____ OCCUPATION

_____ ADVERB

_____ NOUN

Life under the sea is full of wonder and _____ —especially when

PLURAL NOUN

you're a mermaid and a/an _____ underwater princess like me! I

ADJECTIVE

live on the ocean floor in a/an _____ castle made of coral

ADJECTIVE

_____ . My dad is King _____ , ruler of the

PLURAL NOUN · PERSON IN ROOM (MALE)

entire _____ . My friends are fish, dolphins, and underwater

NOUN

_____ . We spend our days exploring _____ reefs

PLURAL NOUN · NOUN

and searching for sunken _____ . Sometimes I wonder what it

PLURAL NOUN

would be like to _____ on land. I've heard that people there have

VERB

_____ instead of fins. And that they _____

PART OF THE BODY (PLURAL) · VERB

around from place to place in motorized _____ and wear

PLURAL NOUN

_____ _____ on their _____ .

ADJECTIVE · PLURAL NOUN · PART OF THE BODY (PLURAL)

Someday I hope to visit this place so I can meet a handsome _____

OCCUPATION

and fall _____ in love. That would be a mermaid's _____

ADVERB · NOUN

come true!

MAD LIBS® is fun to play with friends, but you can also play it by yourself! To begin with, DO NOT look at the story on the page below. Fill in the blanks on this page with the words called for. Then, using the words you have selected, fill in the blank spaces in the story.

Now you've created your own hilarious MAD LIBS® game!

RAPUNZEL'S HAIR TIPS

ADJECTIVE _____

NOUN _____

PLURAL NOUN _____

PLURAL NOUN _____

NOUN _____

NUMBER _____

PLURAL NOUN _____

ADJECTIVE _____

ADJECTIVE _____

NOUN _____

NUMBER _____

PART OF THE BODY _____

ADJECTIVE _____

PERSON IN ROOM (MALE) _____

ADJECTIVE _____

MAD LIBS
RAPUNZEL'S HAIR TIPS

Hi, my dears. Rapunzel here. As you may know, I'm famous for my long and

_____ hair. How do I maintain it? Here are some tips that will
ADJECTIVE

help you get a beautiful _____ just like mine:
NOUN

• Use shampoo made from all-natural _____ and
PLURAL NOUN

_____ .
PLURAL NOUN

• Be sure to groom your hair with a fine-tooth _____ for
NOUN

_____ hours a day.
NUMBER

• Eat plenty of fresh _____: The natural oils will give your hair
PLURAL NOUN

a/an _____ sheen and _____ body.
ADJECTIVE   ADJECTIVE

• Wash your _____ no more than _____ times a day.
NOUN   NUMBER

Otherwise, it will get dry and you may look like you stuck your

_____ in an electric socket.
PART OF THE BODY

Follow these _____ tips and Prince _____ will
ADJECTIVE   PERSON IN ROOM (MALE)

be able to climb up your hair and rescue you if you should happen to be

imprisoned in a/an _____ tower!
ADJECTIVE

MAD LIBS® is fun to play with friends, but you can also play it by yourself! To begin with, DO NOT look at the story on the page below. Fill in the blanks on this page with the words called for. Then, using the words you have selected, fill in the blank spaces in the story.

Now you've created your own hilarious MAD LIBS® game!

A NEW FAIRY TALE

ADJECTIVE _____

PERSON IN ROOM (FEMALE) _____

NOUN _____

A PLACE _____

ADJECTIVE _____

PART OF THE BODY _____

ADJECTIVE _____

ADJECTIVE _____

ADJECTIVE _____

NOUN _____

NOUN _____

NOUN _____

VERB _____

PLURAL NOUN _____

NOUN _____

ADJECTIVE _____

MAD LIBS

A NEW FAIRY TALE

Once upon a time, there lived a/an _____ , young girl named
          ADJECTIVE

_____ who lived in a little wooden _____
PERSON IN ROOM (FEMALE)   NOUN

by (the) _____ . She was a/an _____ child,
          A PLACE   ADJECTIVE

always willing to lend a/an _____ to the _____
                            PART OF THE BODY   ADJECTIVE

villagers. She was small and _____ but worked very hard.
                              ADJECTIVE

Then, one day, she happened upon a/an _____ frog. To her
                                        ADJECTIVE

surprise, this little slimy _____ could talk! In a deep, croaky
                              NOUN

voice, it said, "I will grant you three wishes, but then you must give me a/an

_____ on the lips." She agreed. And for her first wish, she
     NOUN

asked for a new _____ for her parents to live in. For her
                    NOUN

second, she wished to be able to _____ like a bird. For her
                                      VERB

final wish, she asked for all the _____ in the world! And it
                                  PLURAL NOUN

all came to pass just as the frog said. The girl kissed the frog and he suddenly

turned into a handsome, young _____ . She couldn't
                                    NOUN

believe her _____ luck!
              ADJECTIVE

MAD LIBS® is fun to play with friends, but you can also play it by yourself! To begin with, DO NOT look at the story on the page below. Fill in the blanks on this page with the words called for. Then, using the words you have selected, fill in the blank spaces in the story.

Now you've created your own hilarious MAD LIBS® game!

PINOCCHIO'S DIARY

_____ NOUN

_____ ADJECTIVE

_____ NOUN

_____ ADJECTIVE

_____ NOUN

_____ NOUN

_____ PERSON IN ROOM (MALE)

_____ ADJECTIVE

_____ ADJECTIVE

_____ ADVERB

_____ NOUN

_____ PART OF THE BODY (PLURAL)

_____ PART OF THE BODY

_____ NUMBER

_____ NOUN

MAD LIBS®
PINOCCHIO'S DIARY

6:20 A.M.: Woke up this morning, looked at my face in the

_____ , and I was still nothing but a/an _____
        NOUN   ADJECTIVE

puppet carved out of _____ . Depressed, went back to sleep.
                            NOUN

6:50 A.M.: Awakened by a/an _____ fairy. She said that if I
                                  ADJECTIVE

want to become a real _____ , I must have a conscience.
                              NOUN

Then she disappeared into thin _____ .
                                      NOUN

7:12 A.M.: A cricket named _____ visited me. He said that a
                              PERSON IN ROOM (MALE)

boy with a good conscience can tell right from _____ , and
                                                      ADJECTIVE

he always speaks the _____ truth. He added that if I lie, it
                            ADJECTIVE

will become _____ apparent to everyone.
                  ADVERB

7:30 A.M.: Excited, I woke up my dad, Geppetto, and told him that I had

become a real _____ , just like he always wanted. Geppetto's
                    NOUN

_____ filled with tears.
PART OF THE BODY (PLURAL)

8:30 A.M.: Geppetto asked if I would like to go to school. I said yes.

Suddenly my _____ grew _____ inches. I took a solemn
              PART OF THE BODY   NUMBER

_____ never to lie again.
      NOUN

MAD LIBS® is fun to play with friends, but you can also play it by yourself! To begin with, DO NOT look at the story on the page below. Fill in the blanks on this page with the words called for. Then, using the words you have selected, fill in the blank spaces in the story.

Now you've created your own hilarious MAD LIBS® game!

MAGIC WAND FOR SALE

OCCUPATION _____

NOUN _____

PLURAL NOUN _____

PLURAL NOUN _____

PLURAL NOUN _____

PERSON IN ROOM (MALE) _____

PLURAL NOUN _____

PLURAL NOUN _____

ADJECTIVE _____

NUMBER _____

PLURAL NOUN _____

ADJECTIVE _____

ADJECTIVE _____

PLURAL NOUN _____

MAD LIBS®
MAGIC WAND FOR SALE

Are you a wizard, a fairy godmother, or a/an _____ looking for
<u>OCCUPATION</u>

a magic _____ that can do it all? Do you need to turn frogs
<u>NOUN</u>

into _____ or make _____ fly or have an
<u>PLURAL NOUN</u>   <u>PLURAL NOUN</u>

evil witch vanish into a puff of smoke? Well, look no further! This is the

wand that can do anything! That's right—the Wandinator 2000 is here!

Handcrafted from the finest _____ , this is the same wand that
<u>PLURAL NOUN</u>

the famous wizard _____ uses. With the Wandinator 2000,
<u>PERSON IN ROOM (MALE)</u>

you, too, can change a pile of worthless _____ into valuable
<u>PLURAL NOUN</u>

_____ . Tired of wands that are _____ and wear
<u>PLURAL NOUN</u>   <u>ADJECTIVE</u>

out too fast? The Wandinator 2000 is guaranteed to last _____
<u>NUMBER</u>

years or your _____ back! Act now and get a free _____
<u>PLURAL NOUN</u>   <u>ADJECTIVE</u>

carrying case. Don't miss this _____ opportunity. Buy it now!
<u>ADJECTIVE</u>

Gold, silver, _____ , and credit cards accepted.
<u>PLURAL NOUN</u>

MAD LIBS® is fun to play with friends, but you can also play it by yourself! To begin with, DO NOT look at the story on the page below. Fill in the blanks on this page with the words called for. Then, using the words you have selected, fill in the blank spaces in the story.

Now you've created your own hilarious MAD LIBS® game!

SO YOU WANT
TO BE A VILLAIN?

ADJECTIVE _____

NOUN _____

PLURAL NOUN _____

ADJECTIVE _____

PERSON IN ROOM _____

PERSON IN ROOM _____

NOUN _____

ADJECTIVE _____

PLURAL NOUN _____

PERSON IN ROOM _____

CELEBRITY _____

PLURAL NOUN _____

OCCUPATION (PLURAL) _____

ADJECTIVE _____

ADJECTIVE _____

ADJECTIVE _____

It is not easy being a/an _____ villain in a sea of fairy
                              ADJECTIVE

_____ -mothers, magical _____ , and
         NOUN   PLURAL NOUN

_____ princes and princesses. To be a really successful villain
      ADJECTIVE

like Count _____ or _____ the Wicked
            PERSON IN ROOM   PERSON IN ROOM

_____ will take practice and the right tools. First, you'll
      NOUN

need a really _____ laugh, since you have to cackle alongside
                 ADJECTIVE

the most evil witches and horrible _____ . It is also
                                        PLURAL NOUN

recommended that you hire some evil henchmen like _____
                                                      PERSON IN ROOM

or _____ to help you steal golden _____ or
      CELEBRITY   PLURAL NOUN

kidnap wealthy _____ . And, of course, you'll need a
                 OCCUPATION (PLURAL)

place to hide out. A dark, _____ cave is good, but so are
                              ADJECTIVE

_____ alleys. Follow these directions and you will certainly
      ADJECTIVE

become a really _____ , world-famous villain!
                   ADJECTIVE

MAD LIBS® is fun to play with friends, but you can also play it by yourself! To begin with, DO NOT look at the story on the page below. Fill in the blanks on this page with the words called for. Then, using the words you have selected, fill in the blank spaces in the story.

Now you've created your own hilarious MAD LIBS® game!

THE PRINCESS
AND THE PEA

PERSON IN ROOM (MALE) _____

PERSON IN ROOM (FEMALE) _____

ADJECTIVE _____

ADJECTIVE _____

NOUN _____

NOUN _____

NOUN _____

ADJECTIVE _____

NOUN _____

ADJECTIVE _____

ADJECTIVE _____

ADVERB _____

A PLACE _____

MAD LIBS
THE PRINCESS AND THE PEA

There once was a prince named _____ . His mother,

PERSON IN ROOM (MALE)

Queen _____ , summoned many princesses to meet him.

PERSON IN ROOM (FEMALE)

But none were _____ enough. Then one night, during

ADJECTIVE

a/an _____ storm, the prince heard a loud knock at the

ADJECTIVE

_____ . He opened it, and there stood a fair maiden,

NOUN

soaking wet but as beautiful as a summer's _____ . It was

NOUN

love at first _____ . The girl said she was a princess, but the

NOUN

queen was doubtful. Luckily, she had a way to make sure. She took the girl to

a/an _____ bedroom where she had piled mattress upon

ADJECTIVE

mattress until they almost reached the ceiling. Underneath, she placed a tiny

_____ . If the young woman felt the pea through the

NOUN

mattresses, she was really a/an _____ princess. Sure enough,

ADJECTIVE

the next morning, the maiden complained that she was unable to sleep

because the _____ bed was so uncomfortable. The prince

ADJECTIVE

married her and they lived _____ ever after in (the)

ADVERB

_____ .

A PLACE

ROCK 'N' ROLL
MAD LIBS

by Roger Price and Leonard Stern

PSS!

PRICE STERN SLOAN

An Imprint of Penguin Group (USA) Inc.

PRICE STERN SLOAN
Published by the Penguin Group
Penguin Group (USA) Inc., 375 Hudson Street, New York, New York 10014, USA
Penguin Group (Canada), 90 Eglinton Avenue East, Suite 700, Toronto, Ontario M4P 2Y3, Canada
(a division of Pearson Penguin Canada Inc.)
Penguin Books Ltd, 80 Strand, London WC2R 0RL, England
Penguin Group Ireland, 25 St. Stephen's Green, Dublin 2, Ireland
(a division of Penguin Books Ltd.)
Penguin Group (Australia), 250 Camberwell Road, Camberwell, Victoria 3124, Australia
(a division of Pearson Australia Group Pty. Ltd.)
Penguin Books India Pvt. Ltd, 11 Community Centre, Panchsheel Park, New Delhi—110 017, India
Penguin Group (NZ), 67 Apollo Drive, Rosedale, North Shore 0632, New Zealand
(a division of Pearson New Zealand Ltd.)
Penguin Books (South Africa) (Pty.) Ltd., 24 Sturdee Avenue,
Rosebank, Johannesburg 2196, South Africa

Penguin Books Ltd., Registered Offices:
80 Strand, London WC2R 0RL, England

Published by Price Stern Sloan,
a division of Penguin Young Readers Group,
345 Hudson Street, New York, New York 10014.

Mad About Mad Libs published in 2013 by Price Stern Sloan,
a division of Penguin Young Readers Group, 345 Hudson Street, New York, New York 10014.

Mad About Mad Libs ISBN 978-0-8431-7604-9

1 3 5 7 9 10 8 6 4 2

INSTRUCTIONS

MAD LIBS® is a game for people who don't like games!
It can be played by one, two, three, four, or forty.

• RIDICULOUSLY SIMPLE DIRECTIONS

In this tablet you will find stories containing blank spaces where words are left out. One player, the **READER**, selects one of these stories. The **READER** does not tell anyone what the story is about. Instead, he/she asks the other players, the **WRITERS**, to give him/her words. These words are used to fill in the blank spaces in the story.

• TO PLAY

The **READER** asks each **WRITER** in turn to call out a word—an adjective or a noun or whatever the space calls for—and uses them to fill in the blank spaces in the story. The result is a **MAD LIBS**® game.

When the **READER** then reads the completed **MAD LIBS**® game to the other players, they will discover that they have written a story that is fantastic, screamingly funny, shocking, silly, crazy, or just plain dumb—depending upon which words each **WRITER** called out.

• EXAMPLE (*Before* and *After*)

"_____!" he said _____
        EXCLAMATION   ADVERB

as he jumped into his convertible _____ and
                                                      NOUN

drove off with his _____ wife.
                              ADJECTIVE

"____*Ouch*____!" he said ____*stupidly*____
        EXCLAMATION   ADVERB

as he jumped into his convertible ____*cat*____ and
                                                      NOUN

drove off with his ____*brave*____ wife.
                              ADJECTIVE

QUICK REVIEW

In case you have forgotten what adjectives, adverbs, nouns, and verbs are, here is a quick review:

An **ADJECTIVE** describes something or somebody. *Lumpy, soft, ugly, messy,* and *short* are adjectives.

An **ADVERB** tells how something is done. It modifies a verb and usually ends in "ly." *Modestly, stupidly, greedily,* and *carefully* are adverbs.

A **NOUN** is the name of a person, place, or thing. *Sidewalk, umbrella, bridle, bathtub,* and *nose* are nouns.

A **VERB** is an action word. *Run, pitch, jump,* and *swim* are verbs. Put the verbs in past tense if the directions say PAST TENSE. *Ran, pitched, jumped,* and *swam* are verbs in the past tense.

When we ask for **A PLACE**, we mean any sort of place: a country or city *(Spain, Cleveland)* or a room *(bathroom, kitchen).*

An **EXCLAMATION** or **SILLY WORD** is any sort of funny sound, gasp, grunt, or outcry, like *Wow!, Ouch!, Whomp!, Ick!,* and *Gadzooks!*

When we ask for specific words, like a **NUMBER**, a **COLOR**, an **ANIMAL**, or a **PART OF THE BODY**, we mean a word that is one of those things, like *seven, blue, horse,* or *head.*

When we ask for a **PLURAL**, it means more than one. For example, *cat* pluralized is *cats.*

MAD LIBS® is fun to play with friends, but you can also play it by yourself! To begin with, DO NOT look at the story on the page below. Fill in the blanks on this page with the words called for. Then, using the words you have selected, fill in the blank spaces in the story.

Now you've created your own hilarious MAD LIBS® game!

FAMILY ROCK BAND

ADJECTIVE _____

LAST NAME _____

ADJECTIVE _____

NOUN _____

ADJECTIVE _____

PLURAL NOUN _____

NOUN _____

ADJECTIVE _____

PLURAL NOUN _____

NOUN _____

ADJECTIVE _____

PLURAL NOUN _____

ADJECTIVE _____

ADJECTIVE _____

NOUN _____

ADVERB _____

LETTER OF THE ALPHABET _____

NOUN _____

MAD LIBS®
FAMILY ROCK BAND

I don't come from your average _____ family. That's because
                                    ADJECTIVE

we're all part of the _____ Family rock band and we lead a very
                        LAST NAME

_____ life. For example, by not shaving his _____
   ADJECTIVE   NOUN

every morning, my dad saves enough time to practice the _____
                                                            ADJECTIVE

drums. My brother doesn't participate in extracurricular _____
                                                            PLURAL NOUN

at school because he plays the electric _____. My _____
                                            NOUN   ADJECTIVE

sister doesn't have time to date _____ because she sings lead
                                    PLURAL NOUN

vocals and practices for four or five hours every _____. When
                                                        NOUN

I'm not writing our _____ songs, I'm tickling the _____
                        ADJECTIVE   PLURAL NOUN

on the keyboard, so I don't have any free time either. Finally, Mom is our

_____ manager. She books our band to play at weddings,
   ADJECTIVE

_____ sixteens, and _____ mitzvahs. Maybe
   ADJECTIVE   NOUN

someday, if we practice _____ enough, we'll get to make a music
                            ADVERB

video for _____-TV and play sold-out shows at Madison
            LETTER OF THE ALPHABET

Square _____!
           NOUN

MAD LIBS® is fun to play with friends, but you can also play it by yourself! To begin with, DO NOT look at the story on the page below. Fill in the blanks on this page with the words called for. Then, using the words you have selected, fill in the blank spaces in the story.

Now you've created your own hilarious MAD LIBS® game!

TEST YOUR MUSICAL IQ

_____ NOUN

_____ ADJECTIVE

_____ ADJECTIVE

_____ OCCUPATION

_____ ADJECTIVE

_____ PERSON IN ROOM

_____ ADJECTIVE

_____ ADJECTIVE

_____ VERB

_____ NOUN

_____ VERB

_____ SILLY WORD

_____ NOUN

_____ ADVERB

_____ NOUN

_____ NOUN

MAD LIBS®
TEST YOUR MUSICAL IQ

Think you're a true music _____? Test your knowledge in the
NOUN

_____ quiz below!
ADJECTIVE

1. Which _____ singer and part-time _____
ADJECTIVE   OCCUPATION

recently won the Grammy for "_____ Album of the Year"?
ADJECTIVE

Answer: _____
PERSON IN ROOM

2. What is the _____ definition of the musical term *allegro*?
ADJECTIVE

Answer: _____
ADJECTIVE

3. What was the first rock 'n' _____ song to hit number one on
VERB

the _____ charts?
NOUN

Answer: "_____ Around the Clock"
VERB

4. What was Wolfgang _____ Mozart's last opera?
SILLY WORD

Answer: *The Magic* _____
NOUN

5. Which song is always sung _____ prior to American sporting
ADVERB

events like _____-ball games?
NOUN

Answer: "The Star-Spangled _____"
NOUN

MAD LIBS® is fun to play with friends, but you can also play it by yourself! To begin with, DO NOT look at the story on the page below. Fill in the blanks on this page with the words called for. Then, using the words you have selected, fill in the blank spaces in the story.

Now you've created your own hilarious MAD LIBS® game!

INTERVIEW WITH A ROCK STAR

ADJECTIVE _____

PLURAL NOUN _____

NOUN _____

ADJECTIVE _____

ADJECTIVE _____

A PLACE _____

ADJECTIVE _____

NOUN _____

NOUN _____

NOUN _____

PLURAL NOUN _____

PLURAL NOUN _____

ADJECTIVE _____

PLURAL NOUN _____

NOUN _____

The famous Johnny Rockstar, from the _____ band The

_____ ADJECTIVE

_____, recently gave an exclusive interview to the

PLURAL NOUN

_____ *City Times*. Here's how it went:

NOUN

Interviewer: When did you get your first _____ break?

ADJECTIVE

Rockstar: The band had just finished playing at a/an _____

ADJECTIVE

lounge in (the) _____ when a/an _____

A PLACE   ADJECTIVE

music executive walked up to me and said, "Hey, kid. You've got real

_____ quality!" She signed the band to a three-_____

NOUN   NOUN

deal with her record company! We couldn't believe our _____!

NOUN

Interviewer: What advice would you give to aspiring young _____?

PLURAL NOUN

Rockstar: Don't ever let go of your _____.

PLURAL NOUN

Interviewer: What's the best part of your _____ rock star life?

ADJECTIVE

Rockstar: Getting mail from my loyal and devoted _____. Oh,

PLURAL NOUN

and seeing my _____ in the newspaper!

NOUN

MAD LIBS® is fun to play with friends, but you can also play it by yourself! To begin with, DO NOT look at the story on the page below. Fill in the blanks on this page with the words called for. Then, using the words you have selected, fill in the blank spaces in the story.

Now you've created your own hilarious MAD LIBS® game!

MY FIRST ROCK CONCERT

VERB ENDING IN "ING" _____

PLURAL NOUN _____

PART OF THE BODY _____

ADVERB _____

ADVERB _____

PLURAL NOUN _____

ADJECTIVE _____

PART OF THE BODY (PLURAL) _____

ADVERB _____

ADJECTIVE _____

ADJECTIVE _____

ADJECTIVE _____

SAME ADJECTIVE _____

NOUN _____

ADJECTIVE _____

NOUN _____

PART OF THE BODY _____

MAD LIBS
MY FIRST ROCK CONCERT

The first band I ever saw in concert was the _____
<u>VERB ENDING IN "ING"</u>

_____. Before the show began, I stood shoulder-to-
<u>PLURAL NOUN</u>

_____ with the crowd as we _____ awaited the
<u>PART OF THE BODY</u>   <u>ADVERB</u>

band's arrival. When they _____ walked onstage, everyone cheered
<u>ADVERB</u>

like wild _____. Then they began to play their _____
<u>PLURAL NOUN</u>   <u>ADJECTIVE</u>

music, and I sang along at the top of my _____. When they
<u>PART OF THE BODY (PLURAL)</u>

finished and _____ left the stage, I felt _____
<u>ADVERB</u>   <u>ADJECTIVE</u>

because it was over. But then, to my _____ surprise, the crowd
<u>ADJECTIVE</u>

began yelling for more. The band came back and played their hit song,

" _____, _____ Baby"! I was as happy as a/an
<u>ADJECTIVE</u>   <u>SAME ADJECTIVE</u>

_____. To make sure I'd remember this _____
<u>NOUN</u>   <u>ADJECTIVE</u>

experience for the rest of my _____, I bought myself a T-shirt
<u>NOUN</u>

with a picture of the lead singer's _____ on it!
<u>PART OF THE BODY</u>

From ROCK 'N' ROLL MAD LIBS®. Copyright © 2010 by Price Stern Sloan,
a division of Penguin Young Readers Group, 345 Hudson Street, New York, NY 10014.

CLASSICAL GENIUS

CELEBRITY _____

ADJECTIVE _____

NOUN _____

ADJECTIVE _____

PLURAL NOUN _____

LAST NAME _____

ADJECTIVE _____

PLURAL NOUN _____

PLURAL NOUN _____

ADJECTIVE _____

PLURAL NOUN _____

NOUN _____

PLURAL NOUN _____

ADJECTIVE _____

LETTER OF THE ALPHABET _____

MAD LIBS® is fun to play with friends, but you can also play it by yourself! To begin with, DO NOT look at the story on the page below. Fill in the blanks on this page with the words called for. Then, using the words you have selected, fill in the blank spaces in the story.

Now you've created your own hilarious MAD LIBS® game!

MAD LIBS®
CLASSICAL GENIUS

Are you familiar with the _____ Effect? It's a/an
_{CELEBRITY}

_____ theory that says people should listen to classical music to
_{ADJECTIVE}

become smarter than the average _____. This hypothesis was
_{NOUN}

first proposed by some _____ scientists who asked several
_{ADJECTIVE}

_____ to listen to a few minutes of music by musical greats
_{PLURAL NOUN}

such as Mozart, Bach, Beethoven, and _____. Then they gave
_{LAST NAME}

their subjects a/an _____ test. The results showed that the
_{ADJECTIVE}

_____ who listened to the music scored better than the
_{PLURAL NOUN}

_____ who didn't. Apparently, the _____
_{PLURAL NOUN} _{ADJECTIVE}

theory is correct: Listening to classical music does help you memorize

_____, sharpen your _____ skills, and prevent
_{PLURAL NOUN} _{NOUN}

_____. So the next time you have a/an _____ test
_{PLURAL NOUN} _{ADJECTIVE}

at school, just try listening to Beethoven before you take the exam—you're

almost guaranteed to get a/an _____!
_{LETTER OF THE ALPHABET}

MAD LIBS® is fun to play with friends, but you can also play it by yourself! To begin with, DO NOT look at the story on the page below. Fill in the blanks on this page with the words called for. Then, using the words you have selected, fill in the blank spaces in the story.

Now you've created your own hilarious MAD LIBS® game!

ON THE ROAD

PERSON IN ROOM _____

PLURAL NOUN _____

NOUN _____

A PLACE _____

A PLACE _____

ADJECTIVE _____

CELEBRITY _____

NOUN _____

NUMBER _____

PLURAL NOUN _____

ADJECTIVE _____

ADJECTIVE _____

PART OF THE BODY (PLURAL) _____

ANIMAL _____

NOUN _____

PART OF THE BODY _____

MAD LIBS®
ON THE ROAD

Dear Diary,

It's day thirty-two of my "Best of _____" World Tour. I've been
                                              PERSON IN ROOM

to so many cities and met so many _____ that I don't even
                                          PLURAL NOUN

remember where I am from one _____ to the next. At tonight's
                                    NOUN

concert in (the) _____, I accidentally shouted into the
                      A PLACE

microphone, "Hello, (the) _____—how are you feelin' tonight?"
                                A PLACE

Oops! Tonight I have to be sure to get a/an _____ night's sleep
                                                  ADJECTIVE

because tomorrow I have an early TV interview with _____ on
                                                          CELEBRITY

the _____ *Show*, then I have to spend _____ hours
        NOUN   NUMBER

signing _____ for _____ fans, and my afternoon is
            PLURAL NOUN   ADJECTIVE

totally booked with seven _____ radio interviews. I'll keep
                                ADJECTIVE

my _____ crossed that I am able to take a quick
        PART OF THE BODY (PLURAL)

_____-nap before we perform our final _____ at
    ANIMAL   NOUN

the amphitheater here in—wait, where are we again? I can hardly keep my

_____ on straight. Help!
    PART OF THE BODY

From ROCK 'N' ROLL MAD LIBS®. Copyright © 2010 by Price Stern Sloan,
a division of Penguin Young Readers Group, 345 Hudson Street, New York, NY 10014.

MAD LIBS MUSIC OFFER

VERB _____

ADJECTIVE _____

PLURAL NOUN _____

ADJECTIVE _____

PLURAL NOUN _____

VERB _____

PLURAL NOUN _____

ADJECTIVE _____

ADJECTIVE _____

VERB _____

ADJECTIVE _____

ADJECTIVE _____

ADJECTIVE _____

PLURAL NOUN _____

PERSON IN ROOM _____

NOUN _____

NUMBER _____

ADJECTIVE _____

PLURAL NOUN _____

MAD LIBS® is fun to play with friends, but you can also play it by yourself! To begin with, DO NOT look at the story on the page below. Fill in the blanks on this page with the words called for. Then, using the words you have selected, fill in the blank spaces in the story.

Now you've created your own hilarious MAD LIBS® game!

MAD LIBS®
MAD LIBS MUSIC OFFER

They taught us how to love. They taught us how to _____. And
 VERB

now they're back! This all-new collection of _____ *Ballads* is
 ADJECTIVE

guaranteed to knock your _____ off! This _____
 PLURAL NOUN ADJECTIVE

CD set contains twenty of the hottest mega-_____ of all time,
 PLURAL NOUN

including "Don't _____" by _____ N' Roses,
 VERB PLURAL NOUN

"_____ Enough" by _____ Yankees, and, for all you
 ADJECTIVE ADJECTIVE

romantics out there, the unforgettable "To _____ with You" by
 VERB

Mr. _____, for when you're feeling _____ on a
 ADJECTIVE ADJECTIVE

Saturday night. But wait—there's more! This _____ collection
 ADJECTIVE

comes with a bonus DVD of music _____, featuring everything
 PLURAL NOUN

_____ ever recorded! Yes, _____ fans, for only
PERSON IN ROOM NOUN

_____ dollars and ninety-five cents, you can own all of these
 NUMBER

_____ singles from yesteryear. Call now! This collection is
 ADJECTIVE

not sold in _____!
 PLURAL NOUN

MAD LIBS® is fun to play with friends, but you can also play it by yourself! To begin with, DO NOT look at the story on the page below. Fill in the blanks on this page with the words called for. Then, using the words you have selected, fill in the blank spaces in the story.

Now you've created your own hilarious MAD LIBS® game!

SING ALONG, PART 1

_____ ADJECTIVE

_____ PLURAL NOUN

_____ NOUN

_____ ADJECTIVE

_____ ADJECTIVE

_____ TYPE OF LIQUID

_____ NOUN

_____ NOUN

_____ NOUN

_____ ANIMAL

_____ ARTICLE OF CLOTHING

_____ EXCLAMATION

_____ NOUN

_____ NOUN

_____ NOUN

_____ NOUN

MAD LIBS
SING ALONG, PART 1

You may be a/an _____ musical expert now, but do you
                          ADJECTIVE

remember some of the first _____ you ever learned to sing? Let's
                                  PLURAL NOUN

take a walk down _____ lane as we recall some _____
                        NOUN   ADJECTIVE

children's songs, Mad Libs style!

1. The itsy-_____ spider went up the _____ spout.
              ADJECTIVE   TYPE OF LIQUID

   Down came the rain and washed the _____ out. Out came
                                              NOUN

   the _____ and dried up all the rain and the itsy-bitsy spider
            NOUN

   went up the _____ again.
                      NOUN

2. All around the mulberry _____ , the _____
                                  NOUN   ANIMAL

   chased the weasel. The monkey stopped to pull up his _____.
                                                              ARTICLE OF CLOTHING

   "_____!" goes the weasel.
      EXCLAMATION

3. Rock-a-bye, _____, in the treetop. When the _____
                    NOUN   NOUN

   blows, the cradle will rock. When the _____ breaks, the
                                                NOUN

   cradle will fall, and down will come baby, _____, and all.
                                                      NOUN

SING ALONG, PART 2

ADJECTIVE _____

NOUN _____

NOUN _____

VERB (PAST TENSE) _____

NOUN _____

NOUN _____

NOUN _____

TYPE OF FOOD _____

NOUN _____

ADJECTIVE _____

ADJECTIVE _____

PLURAL NOUN _____

NOUN _____

NOUN _____

ADJECTIVE _____

ADJECTIVE _____

MAD LIBS® is fun to play with friends, but you can also play it by yourself! To begin with, DO NOT look at the story on the page below. Fill in the blanks on this page with the words called for. Then, using the words you have selected, fill in the blank spaces in the story.

Now you've created your own hilarious MAD LIBS® game!

MAD LIBS®
SING ALONG, PART 2

Now let's see how many of these _____ patriotic songs you know:
ADJECTIVE

1. My _____ 'tis of thee, sweet _____ of liberty, of
   NOUN   NOUN

   thee I sing. Land where my fathers _____, land of the
                                        VERB (PAST TENSE)

   pilgrims' pride, from every mountainside, let _____ ring!
                                                   NOUN

2. Yankee-Doodle went to town, a-riding on a/an _____. Stuck
                                                   NOUN

   a feather in his _____ and called it _____.
                      NOUN   TYPE OF FOOD

   Yankee-Doodle, keep it up! Yankee-Doodle dandy. Mind the music

   and the _____, and with the girls be _____!
             NOUN   ADJECTIVE

3. And the rockets' _____ glare, the _____
                      ADJECTIVE   PLURAL NOUN

   bursting in air, gave proof through the night that our _____
                                                            NOUN

   was still there. Oh, say, does that star-spangled _____
                                                        NOUN

   yet wave, o'er the land of the _____ and the home of
                                    ADJECTIVE

   the _____.
         ADJECTIVE

MAD LIBS® is fun to play with friends, but you can also play it by yourself! To begin with, DO NOT look at the story on the page below. Fill in the blanks on this page with the words called for. Then, using the words you have selected, fill in the blank spaces in the story.

Now you've created your own hilarious MAD LIBS® game!

FAN LETTER
TO A POP BAND

LAST NAME _____

CELEBRITY _____

NUMBER _____

ADJECTIVE _____

PLURAL NOUN _____

ADJECTIVE _____

NOUN _____

VERB ENDING IN "ING" _____

ADJECTIVE _____

A PLACE _____

ADJECTIVE _____

NOUN _____

PLURAL NOUN _____

PLURAL NOUN _____

ADVERB _____

ADJECTIVE _____

PERSON IN ROOM _____

MAD LIBS®
FAN LETTER
TO A POP BAND

Dear _____ Brothers,
        LAST NAME

I'm in the sixth grade at _____ Middle School, and I am your
                           CELEBRITY

number _____ fan. I have all of your _____
        NUMBER   ADJECTIVE

albums, but my favorite is *A Whole Lot of* _____. In my opinion,
                                             PLURAL NOUN

the best song you ever recorded is "_____ _____."
                                     ADJECTIVE   NOUN

Whenever it's on the radio, I can't stop _____ to the beat! Now I
                                          VERB ENDING IN "ING"

have some _____ questions for you. First, will you please come
           ADJECTIVE

play a concert in my hometown, (the) _____? Second, when will
                                      A PLACE

you be recording another _____ album? Finally, I read in
                          ADJECTIVE

_____ *Beat* magazine that you guys like to eat fried
 NOUN

_____. I love them, too! I bet we have lots more in common,
 PLURAL NOUN

and if we met, we'd be best _____ forever! Please write back
                             PLURAL NOUN

_____!
 ADVERB

Your devoted and _____ fan,
                  ADJECTIVE

_____
 PERSON IN ROOM

MAD LIBS® is fun to play with friends, but you can also play it by yourself! To begin with, DO NOT look at the story on the page below. Fill in the blanks on this page with the words called for. Then, using the words you have selected, fill in the blank spaces in the story.

Now you've created your own hilarious MAD LIBS® game!

PROFILE OF THE BEATLES

_____ ADJECTIVE

_____ NOUN

_____ A PLACE

_____ NUMBER

_____ NOUN

_____ ADJECTIVE

_____ NOUN

_____ VERB

_____ PERSON IN ROOM

_____ PLURAL NOUN

_____ NOUN

_____ ADJECTIVE

_____ VERB

_____ NOUN

_____ ADVERB

_____ PLURAL NOUN

_____ TYPE OF FOOD

_____ NOUN

MAD LIBS®
PROFILE OF THE BEATLES

The Beatles were not only the most _____ rock 'n' roll band of
                                        ADJECTIVE

all time, they were probably the most critically acclaimed _____
                                                                NOUN

in the history of music. By 1985, this four-member band from (the)

_____ had sold over _____ records internationally—
   A PLACE   NUMBER

more than any other _____ in history. Their _____
                          NOUN   ADJECTIVE

albums include *A Hard Day's* _____, *Let It* _____,
                                   NOUN   VERB

and _____ *Road.* But the Beatles weren't just popular because of
   PERSON IN ROOM

their music. They were fashion _____ and _____
                                   PLURAL NOUN   NOUN

models for their _____ fans. Teenagers tried to dress like them,
                     ADJECTIVE

act like them, and _____ like them. "_____-mania"
                       VERB   NOUN

was a new phrase that referred to the way teenage girls would cry

_____, scream like _____, and faint at Beatles
   ADVERB   PLURAL NOUN

concerts. To sum it up, the Beatles were the biggest thing since sliced

_____, and no band before or since has been able to match their
   TYPE OF FOOD

_____!
   NOUN

MAD LIBS® is fun to play with friends, but you can also play it by yourself! To begin with, DO NOT look at the story on the page below. Fill in the blanks on this page with the words called for. Then, using the words you have selected, fill in the blank spaces in the story.

Now you've created your own hilarious MAD LIBS® game!

ACCEPTANCE SPEECH

EXCLAMATION _____

NOUN _____

NOUN _____

ADJECTIVE _____

NOUN _____

OCCUPATION _____

NOUN _____

ADJECTIVE _____

NOUN _____

OCCUPATION _____

PLURAL NOUN _____

VERB ENDING IN "ING" _____

ADJECTIVE _____

ADJECTIVE _____

NOUN _____

PART OF THE BODY _____

MAD LIBS®
ACCEPTANCE SPEECH

_____! I can't believe I won a/an _____ award! I
   EXCLAMATION   NOUN

have dreamed of this day since I was a little _____. I'd like to
                                                  NOUN

thank all of the _____ people who helped make this
                          ADJECTIVE

_____ become a reality, starting with my _____
    NOUN   OCCUPATION

and, of course, my loving _____ who supported me through
                               NOUN

thick and _____. He believed in my _____ when I
                 ADJECTIVE   NOUN

was just a/an _____ in a small-town diner, struggling to
                        OCCUPATION

make _____ meet. He gave me the strength to keep on
                PLURAL NOUN

_____ no matter what. To the other nominees, I want to say
VERB ENDING IN "ING"

how _____ I feel just to be nominated alongside you. Each one
        ADJECTIVE

of you is a/an _____ artist. It's been a long journey, but worth
                 ADJECTIVE

every _____! Thank you from the bottom of my _____!
    NOUN   PART OF THE BODY

MAD LIBS® is fun to play with friends, but you can also play it by yourself! To begin with, DO NOT look at the story on the page below. Fill in the blanks on this page with the words called for. Then, using the words you have selected, fill in the blank spaces in the story.

Now you've created your own hilarious MAD LIBS® game!

THE JUDGES' DECISION

_____ NOUN

_____ NOUN

_____ PART OF THE BODY

_____ NOUN

_____ ADVERB

_____ PERSON IN ROOM (FEMALE)

_____ ADJECTIVE

_____ PLURAL NOUN

_____ PERSON IN ROOM

_____ ANIMAL

_____ PLURAL NOUN

_____ A PLACE

_____ PERSON IN ROOM

_____ ADJECTIVE

_____ NOUN

_____ NOUN

_____ NOUN

_____ ADJECTIVE

_____ NOUN

MAD LIBS®
THE JUDGES' DECISION

When it was my turn to audition for _____ *Idol,* the reality
                                      NOUN

show where people compete to be the best solo _____, I sang
                                                   NOUN

from the depths of my very _____ . When my song ended,
                            PART OF THE BODY

I could hardly catch my _____ as I _____ awaited
                          NOUN   ADVERB

the judges' response. First, _____ was very kind. She
                             PERSON IN ROOM (FEMALE)

said, "Well the good news is that you look _____, and
                                            ADJECTIVE

you really connected with the _____ in that song." Then
                               PLURAL NOUN

_____ said, "You know, _____, I dug your
PERSON IN ROOM   ANIMAL

_____," and I thought I really had a chance to make it to (the)
PLURAL NOUN

_____! But then mean, old _____ said, "Horrid.
A PLACE   PERSON IN ROOM

Terrible. _____ . You sounded like an animal trapped inside a/an
           ADJECTIVE

_____." I gasped and shouted, "Well, you just don't know
NOUN

anything about _____!" I stormed out of the _____.
                NOUN   NOUN

I was going to make it as a/an _____ singer whether that judge
                                ADJECTIVE

from _____ *Idol* liked me or not!
      NOUN

MAD LIBS® is fun to play with friends, but you can also play it by yourself! To begin with, DO NOT look at the story on the page below. Fill in the blanks on this page with the words called for. Then, using the words you have selected, fill in the blank spaces in the story.

Now you've created your own hilarious MAD LIBS® game!

THE GOOD OL' DAYS

_____ ADJECTIVE

_____ PLURAL NOUN

_____ ADJECTIVE

_____ PLURAL NOUN

_____ NOUN

_____ NOUN

_____ ADJECTIVE

_____ PLURAL NOUN

_____ PLURAL NOUN

_____ PLURAL NOUN

_____ ADJECTIVE

_____ NOUN

_____ PLURAL NOUN

_____ ARTICLE OF CLOTHING (PLURAL)

_____ ADJECTIVE

_____ ADJECTIVE

_____ EXCLAMATION

MAD LIBS®
THE GOOD OL' DAYS

Kids today! Who can figure out their _____ music? Back in
ADJECTIVE

the good old _____, we didn't have _____ mp3s
PLURAL NOUN   ADJECTIVE

and i-_____. We had a/an _____ and a/an
PLURAL NOUN   NOUN

_____ and we'd bang them together to make drums. We didn't
NOUN

have _____ guitars, so we'd use _____ instead. We
ADJECTIVE   PLURAL NOUN

sang about love and _____. We didn't sing angry songs about
PLURAL NOUN

_____. Our music had _____ melodies, but the kids
PLURAL NOUN   ADJECTIVE

nowadays just smash a/an _____ to bits onstage and call it music!
NOUN

They listen to groups like The _____, who wear leather
PLURAL NOUN

_____ and _____ makeup. We used to listen
ARTICLE OF CLOTHING (PLURAL)   ADJECTIVE

to one _____ guy with a banjo and, _____, we liked it!
ADJECTIVE   EXCLAMATION

MAD LIBS® is fun to play with friends, but you can also play it by yourself! To begin with, DO NOT look at the story on the page below. Fill in the blanks on this page with the words called for. Then, using the words you have selected, fill in the blank spaces in the story.

Now you've created your own hilarious MAD LIBS® game!

MUSIC HISTORY: MOZART

_____ ADJECTIVE

_____ PLURAL NOUN

_____ ADJECTIVE

_____ PLURAL NOUN

_____ NOUN

_____ PART OF THE BODY

_____ ADVERB

_____ NOUN

_____ PLURAL NOUN

_____ NOUN

_____ ADJECTIVE

_____ PLURAL NOUN

_____ CELEBRITY

Wolfgang Amadeus Mozart was a/an _____ composer of

ADJECTIVE

the classical era. He created over six hundred musical _____,

PLURAL NOUN

many of which are still considered quite _____. Mozart was

ADJECTIVE

what _____ today call a "child prodigy," which means he had

PLURAL NOUN

talent far beyond that of the average _____. For example, he

NOUN

could compose music inside his _____. He would imagine the

PART OF THE BODY

piece and then play it _____, without writing down a single

ADVERB

_____! Mozart gave concerts for kings, queens, and wealthy

NOUN

_____ who rejoiced in his astonishing _____. This

PLURAL NOUN   NOUN

_____ genius influenced many future _____,

ADJECTIVE   PLURAL NOUN

including Ludwig van Beethoven and _____!

CELEBRITY

ALL ABOUT MUSIC

_____ PLURAL NOUN

_____ ADJECTIVE

_____ ADJECTIVE

_____ NOUN

_____ NOUN

_____ ADJECTIVE

_____ NOUN

_____ NOUN

_____ NOUN

_____ COLOR

_____ PLURAL NOUN

_____ NOUN

_____ ADJECTIVE

_____ PLURAL NOUN

MAD LIBS®
ALL ABOUT MUSIC

There are almost as many types of music as there are _____ in
PLURAL NOUN

the world. Here is a quick guide to some of today's most _____
ADJECTIVE

types of music and how they are interpreted:

1) **Love songs** tend to be slow and _____, allowing the singer to
ADJECTIVE

tell his love, "You are the _____ of my life" or "I want to hold
NOUN

your _____."
NOUN

2) **Country music** usually tells a/an _____ story. Sometimes the
ADJECTIVE

song is about a/an _____ who loses his job, his wife, and even
NOUN

his _____ all at once.
NOUN

3) **The blues** is all about _____ and suffering, and it gets its
NOUN

name from the expression, "feeling _____." Artists express
COLOR

their inner _____ through the blues.
PLURAL NOUN

4) **Rock 'n' roll**'s roots lay mainly in blues, country, gospel, jazz, and

_____. It is performed with _____ energy
NOUN   ADJECTIVE

and has influenced lifestyles and fashion as well as attitudes and

_____.
PLURAL NOUN

STORY OF A
ONE-HIT WONDER

PLURAL NOUN _____

NOUN _____

ADJECTIVE _____

PART OF THE BODY _____

ADJECTIVE _____

ADJECTIVE _____

NOUN _____

ADJECTIVE _____

LAST NAME _____

PLURAL NOUN _____

ADVERB _____

PART OF THE BODY _____

ADJECTIVE _____

NOUN _____

PLURAL NOUN _____

ADJECTIVE _____

A PLACE _____

MAD LIBS® is fun to play with friends, but you can also play it by yourself! To begin with, DO NOT look at the story on the page below. Fill in the blanks on this page with the words called for. Then, using the words you have selected, fill in the blank spaces in the story.

Now you've created your own hilarious MAD LIBS® game!

MAD LIBS®
STORY OF A
ONE-HIT WONDER

The Mighty _____ were a one-_____ wonder,
　　　　　　　　PLURAL NOUN　　　　　　　　　　　　NOUN

famous for their _____ song, "In Your _____."
　　　　　　　　　　ADJECTIVE　　　　　　　　　　　　PART OF THE BODY

Where is this _____ band today? After hitting it big, they
　　　　　　　　ADJECTIVE

started to have _____ creative differences. They went from
　　　　　　　　　ADJECTIVE

superstardom to a/an _____-shattering breakup. The lead singer,
　　　　　　　　　　　NOUN

known for his _____ personality, wanted to change the band's
　　　　　　　　ADJECTIVE

name to _____'s _____. The rest of the band
　　　　　　LAST NAME　　　　PLURAL NOUN

_____ refused. No one could see eye to _____, and
　　ADVERB　　　　　　　　　　　　　　　　　　　　PART OF THE BODY

the bassist decided to leave the _____ band and pursue his
　　　　　　　　　　　　　　　　　ADJECTIVE

lifelong dream of professional _____-weaving. The drummer
　　　　　　　　　　　　　　　NOUN

left to teach music to high school _____. The lead singer was
　　　　　　　　　　　　　　　　　PLURAL NOUN

the only one left. But don't feel too bad—he has now become a/an

_____ Internet sensation with a video of himself playing "Sweet
ADJECTIVE

Home, (the) _____" on the kazoo!
　　　　　　A PLACE

From ROCK 'N' ROLL MAD LIBS®. Copyright © 2010 by Price Stern Sloan,
a division of Penguin Young Readers Group, 345 Hudson Street, New York, NY 10014.

MAD LIBS® is fun to play with friends, but you can also play it by yourself! To begin with, DO NOT look at the story on the page below. Fill in the blanks on this page with the words called for. Then, using the words you have selected, fill in the blank spaces in the story.

Now you've created your own hilarious MAD LIBS® game!

GUESS WHO?

A PLACE _____

NUMBER _____

OCCUPATION _____

NOUN _____

ADJECTIVE _____

PLURAL NOUN _____

PLURAL NOUN _____

PLURAL NOUN _____

NOUN _____

NOUN _____

PLURAL NOUN _____

ADJECTIVE _____

ADJECTIVE _____

She was born in (the) _____, Michigan, in 1942 and started
_____
A PLACE

recording songs when she was only _____ years old. Her
_____
NUMBER

nickname is "The _____ of Soul" and she was the first woman
_____
OCCUPATION

to be inducted into the Rock and Roll _____ of Fame. She has
_____
NOUN

lent her _____ voice to many public events, including the
_____
ADJECTIVE

inaugurations of two American _____. The National Academy
_____
PLURAL NOUN

of Recording Arts and _____ has awarded her seventeen
_____
PLURAL NOUN

Grammy _____, including the prestigious "Living _____
_____   _____
PLURAL NOUN   NOUN

Award" in 1991. One of her greatest hits was called "I Never Loved a/an

_____ the Way I Loved You," but she is best known for her
_____
NOUN

megasmash, "Chain of _____." Just who is this _____
_____   _____
PLURAL NOUN   ADJECTIVE

diva? Of course, it's the truly _____ Aretha Franklin!
_____
ADJECTIVE

MAD LIBS® is fun to play with friends, but you can also play it by yourself! To begin with, DO NOT look at the story on the page below. Fill in the blanks on this page with the words called for. Then, using the words you have selected, fill in the blank spaces in the story.

Now you've created your own hilarious MAD LIBS® game!

ROCK STAR COMMERCIAL

_____ ADJECTIVE

_____ ADJECTIVE

_____ NOUN

_____ ADJECTIVE

_____ NUMBER

_____ ADJECTIVE

_____ ADJECTIVE

_____ PLURAL NOUN

_____ NOUN

_____ NOUN

_____ NOUN

_____ ADJECTIVE

_____ PLURAL NOUN

_____ PART OF THE BODY

_____ NOUN

_____ PLURAL NOUN

_____ ADJECTIVE

_____ ADJECTIVE

_____ ADVERB

_____ SAME ADVERB

_____ ADJECTIVE

_____ NOUN

MAD LIBS®
ROCK STAR COMMERCIAL

This is a/an _____ *rock star TV commercial to be performed by a/an*
        ADJECTIVE

_____ *person in the room:*
  ADJECTIVE

When I'm on tour with my _____, I have to be _____.
               NOUN   ADJECTIVE

That's why I drink at least _____ Rock 'n' Roll Energy Sodas a
                  NUMBER

day. But it's not just for _____ rockers like me, it's a/an
                  ADJECTIVE

_____ pick-me-up for _____ from all walks of life:
  ADJECTIVE   PLURAL NOUN

the stressed-out _____ driver, the overworked computer
               NOUN

_____, or the exhausted high-fashion _____. It's
  NOUN   NOUN

a/an _____ beverage with a special combination of natural
     ADJECTIVE

_____ that vitalizes the mind and _____. I drink
 PLURAL NOUN   PART OF THE BODY

one whenever I record a new _____ or autograph _____
                NOUN   PLURAL NOUN

for my fans. I even have one in the middle of a/an _____
                                 ADJECTIVE

concert to give my _____ singing a boost! People who need to
            ADJECTIVE

perform _____ should drink _____. So try my
       ADVERB   SAME ADVERB

favorite _____ beverage and jump-start your _____
     ADJECTIVE   NOUN

today!

From ROCK 'N' ROLL MAD LIBS®. Copyright © 2010 by Price Stern Sloan,
a division of Penguin Young Readers Group, 345 Hudson Street, New York, NY 10014.

MAD LIBS® is fun to play with friends, but you can also play it by yourself! To begin with, DO NOT look at the story on the page below. Fill in the blanks on this page with the words called for. Then, using the words you have selected, fill in the blank spaces in the story.

Now you've created your own hilarious MAD LIBS® game!

PROM REVIEW

ADJECTIVE _____

PERSON IN ROOM _____

ADJECTIVE _____

PLURAL NOUN _____

ADJECTIVE _____

NOUN _____

PLURAL NOUN _____

ADJECTIVE _____

PLURAL NOUN _____

ADJECTIVE _____

NOUN _____

PERSON IN ROOM (MALE) _____

PERSON IN ROOM (FEMALE) _____

OCCUPATION _____

NUMBER _____

PLURAL NOUN _____

NOUN _____

NOUN _____

MAD LIBS®
PROM REVIEW

Here's a/an _____ review of the senior prom written by
                    ADJECTIVE

_____ for our _____ high school paper:
PERSON IN ROOM   ADJECTIVE

The prom last night was more fun than a barrel of _____!
                                                   PLURAL NOUN

The _____ design committee decorated the gym in an "Under
     ADJECTIVE

the _____" theme, with shimmery blue streamers and inflated
        NOUN

_____ everywhere. It looked absolutely _____.
  PLURAL NOUN   ADJECTIVE

When the band, the Dirty _____, took to the stage, they played
                          PLURAL NOUN

lots of _____ songs including their hit single, "I Wanna Rock
         ADJECTIVE

with a/an _____." During a break in the music, _____
           NOUN   PERSON IN ROOM (MALE)

and _____ were elected Prom King and _____,
     PERSON IN ROOM (FEMALE)   OCCUPATION

and an elegant _____—course dinner was served. It included a
                NUMBER

choice of filet mignon, roasted _____, or poached _____.
                                 PLURAL NOUN   NOUN

When all was said and done, it was truly a/an _____ to
                                               NOUN

remember.

BAND FAN
CLUB MEETING

_____ ADJECTIVE

_____ PLURAL NOUN

_____ PART OF THE BODY

_____ PERSON IN ROOM

_____ ADJECTIVE

_____ NOUN

_____ PERSON IN ROOM

_____ ARTICLE OF CLOTHING (PLURAL)

_____ PART OF THE BODY (PLURAL)

_____ ADJECTIVE

_____ ADJECTIVE

_____ NUMBER

_____ ADJECTIVE

_____ ADJECTIVE

_____ NOUN

_____ EXCLAMATION

MAD LIBS® is fun to play with friends, but you can also play it by yourself! To begin with, DO NOT look at the story on the page below. Fill in the blanks on this page with the words called for. Then, using the words you have selected, fill in the blank spaces in the story.

Now you've created your own hilarious MAD LIBS® game!

MAD LIBS®
BAND FAN
CLUB MEETING

Hear ye, hear ye! This meeting of the _____ _____
                                        ADJECTIVE   PLURAL NOUN

fan club is called to order. First, I would like to give a/an _____
                                                              PART OF THE BODY

-felt thanks to _____ for baking this _____ cake in
                  PERSON IN ROOM   ADJECTIVE

the shape of the band's _____. Next, I'm happy to announce
                              NOUN

that _____ has arrived with what we have all been waiting for:
        PERSON IN ROOM

_____ with pictures of the band's _____
ARTICLE OF CLOTHING (PLURAL)   PART OF THE BODY (PLURAL)

on them! I'm sure we will all wear them with _____ pride.
                                                  ADJECTIVE

Finally, I would like to form a new _____ committee to oversee
                                        ADJECTIVE

the fan letter project. I'm hoping that if we can send at least _____
                                                                    NUMBER

_____ letters to the band, they will consider doing a concert in
   ADJECTIVE

our _____ town—or at least send us an autographed
       ADJECTIVE

_____. All those in favor, say, "_____!"
      NOUN   EXCLAMATION

MAD LIBS®

MAD ABOUT ANIMALS
MAD LIBS

by Roger Price and Leonard Stern

PSS!

PRICE STERN SLOAN

An Imprint of Penguin Group (USA) Inc.

PRICE STERN SLOAN
Published by the Penguin Group
Penguin Group (USA) Inc., 375 Hudson Street, New York, New York 10014, USA
Penguin Group (Canada), 90 Eglinton Avenue East, Suite 700, Toronto, Ontario M4P 2Y3, Canada
(a division of Pearson Penguin Canada Inc.)
Penguin Books Ltd, 80 Strand, London WC2R 0RL, England
Penguin Ireland, 25 St Stephen's Green, Dublin 2, Ireland (a division of Penguin Books Ltd)
Penguin Group (Australia), 707 Collins Street, Melbourne, Victoria 3008, Australia
(a division of Pearson Australia Group Pty Ltd)
Penguin Books India Pvt Ltd, 11 Community Centre, Panchsheel Park, New Delhi—110 017, India
Penguin Group (NZ), 67 Apollo Drive, Rosedale, Auckland 0632, New Zealand
(a division of Pearson New Zealand Ltd)
Penguin Books (South Africa), Rosebank Office Park, 181 Jan Smuts Avenue,
Parktown North 2193, South Africa
Penguin China, B7 Jiaming Center, 27 East Third Ring Road North,
Chaoyang District, Beijing 100020, China

Penguin Books Ltd, Registered Offices: 80 Strand, London WC2R 0RL, England

Mad About Mad Libs published in 2013 by Price Stern Sloan,
a division of Penguin Young Readers Group, 345 Hudson Street, New York, New York 10014.

INSTRUCTIONS

MAD LIBS® is a game for people who don't like games!
It can be played by one, two, three, four, or forty.

• RIDICULOUSLY SIMPLE DIRECTIONS

In this tablet you will find stories containing blank spaces where words are left out. One player, the **READER**, selects one of these stories. The **READER** does not tell anyone what the story is about. Instead, he/she asks the other players, the **WRITERS**, to give him/her words. These words are used to fill in the blank spaces in the story.

• TO PLAY

The **READER** asks each **WRITER** in turn to call out a word—an adjective or a noun or whatever the space calls for—and uses them to fill in the blank spaces in the story. The result is a **MAD LIBS**® game.

When the **READER** then reads the completed **MAD LIBS**® game to the other players, they will discover that they have written a story that is fantastic, screamingly funny, shocking, silly, crazy, or just plain dumb—depending upon which words each **WRITER** called out.

• EXAMPLE (*Before* and *After*)

"_____!" he said _____
      EXCLAMATION   ADVERB

as he jumped into his convertible _____ and
                                            NOUN

drove off with his _____ wife.
                          ADJECTIVE

"_____*Ouch*_____!" he said _____*stupidly*_____
      EXCLAMATION   ADVERB

as he jumped into his convertible _____*cat*_____ and
                                            NOUN

drove off with his _____*brave*_____ wife.
                          ADJECTIVE

MAD LIBS®

QUICK REVIEW

In case you have forgotten what adjectives, adverbs, nouns, and verbs are, here is a quick review:

An **ADJECTIVE** describes something or somebody. *Lumpy, soft, ugly, messy,* and *short* are adjectives.

An **ADVERB** tells how something is done. It modifies a verb and usually ends in "ly." *Modestly, stupidly, greedily,* and *carefully* are adverbs.

A **NOUN** is the name of a person, place, or thing. *Sidewalk, umbrella, bridle, bathtub,* and *nose* are nouns.

A **VERB** is an action word. *Run, pitch, jump,* and *swim* are verbs. Put the verbs in past tense if the directions say PAST TENSE. *Ran, pitched, jumped,* and *swam* are verbs in the past tense.

When we ask for **A PLACE**, we mean any sort of place: a country or city *(Spain, Cleveland)* or a room *(bathroom, kitchen)*.

An **EXCLAMATION** or **SILLY WORD** is any sort of funny sound, gasp, grunt, or outcry, like *Wow!, Ouch!, Whomp!, Ick!,* and *Gadzooks!*

When we ask for specific words, like a **NUMBER**, a **COLOR**, an **ANIMAL**, or a **PART OF THE BODY**, we mean a word that is one of those things, like *seven, blue, horse,* or *head*.

When we ask for a **PLURAL**, it means more than one. For example, *cat* pluralized is *cats*.

DOG'S POINT OF VIEW

_____ PERSON IN ROOM (MALE)

_____ PART OF THE BODY (PLURAL)

_____ NOUN

_____ PART OF THE BODY

_____ ADJECTIVE

_____ ADVERB

_____ NOUN

_____ ADJECTIVE

_____ ADJECTIVE

_____ PART OF THE BODY

_____ PART OF THE BODY (PLURAL)

_____ ADJECTIVE

_____ PLURAL NOUN

_____ PLURAL NOUN

_____ VERB

_____ ADJECTIVE

_____ NOUN

_____ ADJECTIVE

_____ NOUN

MAD LIBS® is fun to play with friends, but you can also play it by yourself! To begin with, DO NOT look at the story on the page below. Fill in the blanks on this page with the words called for. Then, using the words you have selected, fill in the blank spaces in the story.

Now you've created your own hilarious MAD LIBS® game!

MAD LIBS

DOG'S POINT OF VIEW

The minute I saw _____ pucker his _____
PERSON IN ROOM (MALE)   PART OF THE BODY (PLURAL)

and whistle, I knew we were going for a/an _____ ride. I
NOUN

wagged my _____, gave a/an _____ bark, and
PART OF THE BODY   ADJECTIVE

_____ leaped into the back-_____ of the car. As
ADVERB   NOUN

we began our _____ drive through the _____
ADJECTIVE   ADJECTIVE

neighborhood, I stuck my _____ out the window, felt the
PART OF THE BODY

wind in my _____, and took in all the _____
PART OF THE BODY (PLURAL)   ADJECTIVE

smells. We drove past cars, people, and _____ . Then it hit
PLURAL NOUN

me like a ton of _____—we were headed for the dog park! I'd
PLURAL NOUN

get to see and _____ with my _____ girlfriend,
VERB   ADJECTIVE

Fifi, who is a purebred French _____. Yes, sir, despite all the
NOUN

_____ publicity, there's nothing like a dog's life when you
ADJECTIVE

have a generous and caring _____ like mine.
NOUN

From MAD ABOUT ANIMALS MAD LIBS® • Copyright © 2009 by Price Stern Sloan,
an imprint of Penguin Group (USA) Inc., 345 Hudson Street, New York, NY 10014.

MAD LIBS® is fun to play with friends, but you can also play it by yourself! To begin with, DO NOT look at the story on the page below. Fill in the blanks on this page with the words called for. Then, using the words you have selected, fill in the blank spaces in the story.

Now you've created your own hilarious MAD LIBS® game!

POSTCARD FROM A SAFARI

ADJECTIVE _____

ADJECTIVE _____

PLURAL NOUN _____

NOUN _____

PLURAL NOUN _____

TYPE OF LIQUID _____

ADJECTIVE _____

A PLACE _____

NOUN _____

NOUN _____

NOUN _____

PART OF THE BODY _____

ADJECTIVE _____

ADJECTIVE _____

NUMBER _____

NOUN _____

VERB ENDING IN "ING" _____

MAD LIBS®
POSTCARD FROM A SAFARI

Wish you were here on this _____ African safari! We are
                              ADJECTIVE

having the most _____ time of our _____.
                   ADJECTIVE   PLURAL NOUN

Believe it or not, on the first day, we saw a mother _____
                                                          NOUN

and her baby _____ drinking _____
                 PLURAL NOUN   TYPE OF LIQUID

from a watering hole. The second day, we climbed onto the back of a/an

_____ elephant and went through (the) _____,
   ADJECTIVE   A PLACE

and the beauty took my _____ away. But the best—and
                            NOUN

weirdest—part was saved for last. We were deep in the forest when a huge

_____ climbed onto the hood of our _____ and
   NOUN   NOUN

took a swipe at us with its powerful _____. But as this letter
                                       PART OF THE BODY

attests, we survived. All in all, this has been a really _____
                                                              ADJECTIVE

trip. Thankfully you'll be able to share our _____ adventures
                                                 ADJECTIVE

because I've taken more than _____ pictures with my trusty
                                  NUMBER

digital _____. As they say, seeing is _____!
           NOUN   VERB ENDING IN "ING"

AUSTRALIAN WILDLIFE

NOUN _____

ADJECTIVE _____

NOUN _____

PART OF THE BODY (PLURAL) _____

NOUN _____

ADJECTIVE _____

PLURAL NOUN _____

PLURAL NOUN _____

PLURAL NOUN _____

NOUN _____

PLURAL NOUN _____

NOUN _____

NOUN _____

PLURAL NOUN _____

ADJECTIVE _____

MAD LIBS® is fun to play with friends, but you can also play it by yourself! To begin with, DO NOT look at the story on the page below. Fill in the blanks on this page with the words called for. Then, using the words you have selected, fill in the blank spaces in the story.

Now you've created your own hilarious MAD LIBS® game!

MAD LIBS®
AUSTRALIAN WILDLIFE

Australia, also known as the _____ Down Under, is famous
                                  NOUN

for its _____ wildlife. The most famous animal is the kangaroo,
          ADJECTIVE

which carries its baby in a/an _____ on its belly and travels
                                      NOUN

by hopping on its powerful hind _____. The koala is
                                   PART OF THE BODY (PLURAL)

another popular Australian _____. This furry, _____
                                NOUN   ADJECTIVE

creature loves to eat leaves from eucalyptus _____. If you are
                                                  PLURAL NOUN

a bird-watcher, the emu will knock your _____ off. It is a bird
                                            PLURAL NOUN

that has no _____ and cannot fly, but it can run faster than a
                PLURAL NOUN

speeding _____. Perhaps the strangest of all Australian
              NOUN

_____ is the platypus. It has a bill that resembles a duck's
     PLURAL NOUN

_____ and the body of a/an _____. It is one
        NOUN   NOUN

of only two mammals that lay _____ instead of giving
                                    PLURAL NOUN

birth to their young. If you are a nature lover, you must put exotic and

_____ Australia on your places-to-go list!
      ADJECTIVE

MAD LIBS® is fun to play with friends, but you can also play it by yourself! To begin, DO NOT look at the story on the page below. Fill in the blanks on this page with the words called for. Then, using the words you have selected, fill in the blank spaces in the story.

Now you've created your own hilarious MAD LIBS® game!

SCHOOL PET FRET

_____ ADJECTIVE

_____ PERSON IN ROOM (MALE)

_____ ADJECTIVE

_____ NOUN

_____ NOUN

_____ NOUN

_____ PART OF THE BODY

_____ VERB ENDING IN "ING"

_____ ADVERB

_____ NUMBER

_____ PLURAL NOUN

_____ ADJECTIVE

_____ ADJECTIVE

_____ ADJECTIVE

_____ EXCLAMATION

_____ PLURAL NOUN

MAD LIBS®
SCHOOL PET FRET

I recently had the honor of taking our class pet, a/an _____
                                                                ADJECTIVE

rabbit named _____, to my house for the weekend. I carried
              PERSON IN ROOM (MALE)

the little guy in his _____ cage and left him on the kitchen
                          ADJECTIVE

_____ as I went about my afternoon chores of unloading the
        NOUN

_____-washer and taking out the _____. When
        NOUN   NOUN

I came back, my _____ dropped open in shock. He was gone!
                    PART OF THE BODY

My heart was _____ a mile a minute as I _____
                VERB ENDING IN "ING"   ADVERB

ran through the house. I checked every room at least _____
                                                              NUMBER

times. Desperate, I even checked my pile of dirty _____ twice.
                                                        PLURAL NOUN

But I couldn't find him anywhere. Finally I heard a/an _____
                                                              ADJECTIVE

noise and I followed it to the basement. There, right next to the

_____ water heater, was my classroom's precious rabbit—with
    ADJECTIVE

five _____ baby rabbits. _____! The *he* was a
        ADJECTIVE   EXCLAMATION

she! And she had just given birth to a litter of _____!
                                                        PLURAL NOUN

MAD LIBS® is fun to play with friends, but you can also play it by yourself! To begin with, DO NOT look at the story on the page below. Fill in the blanks on this page with the words called for. Then, using the words you have selected, fill in the blank spaces in the story.

Now you've created your own hilarious MAD LIBS® game!

CALLING ALL BIRDS

_____ ADJECTIVE

_____ NOUN

_____ ADJECTIVE

_____ ADJECTIVE

_____ NOUN

_____ ADJECTIVE

_____ PART OF THE BODY

_____ NOUN

_____ ADJECTIVE

_____ PART OF THE BODY

_____ NOUN

_____ ADJECTIVE

_____ NOUN

_____ NOUN

_____ NOUN

MAD LIBS®
CALLING ALL BIRDS

Every bird has a/an _____ song or call—and every talented
                              ADJECTIVE

_____-watcher knows how to imitate them precisely. The
         NOUN

following three _____ birds can be easily imitated by a/an
                        ADJECTIVE

_____ amateur.
        ADJECTIVE

• The yellow-bellied sap _____: A/An _____
                                    NOUN   ADJECTIVE

member of the woodpecker family, its call can be easily reproduced by

squeezing your _____ as tightly as possible and meowing
                    PART OF THE BODY

like a hungry _____ .
                      NOUN

• The pelican: Its _____ call is easy to repeat, provided you
                          ADJECTIVE

stretch your _____ to its fullest length before emitting a
                  PART OF THE BODY

squawk-like _____.
                    NOUN

• The cockatoo: Its vocalization is loud and _____. But
                                                        ADJECTIVE

cockatoos primarily emit a soft, growling _____ when feeding.
                                                    NOUN

They also communicate by drumming a dead _____ with a
                                                      NOUN

stick. And when threatened, they issue an easily duplicated hissing

_____.
        NOUN

MAD LIBS® is fun to play with friends, but you can also play it by yourself! To begin with, DO NOT look at the story on the page below. Fill in the blanks on this page with the words called for. Then, using the words you have selected, fill in the blank spaces in the story.

Now you've created your own hilarious MAD LIBS® game!

FIELD TRIP TO THE ZOO

_____ ADJECTIVE

_____ ADJECTIVE

_____ ADJECTIVE

_____ ADJECTIVE

_____ ADJECTIVE

_____ PLURAL NOUN

_____ PLURAL NOUN

_____ ADJECTIVE

_____ PART OF THE BODY (PLURAL)

_____ NOUN

_____ ADJECTIVE

_____ PLURAL NOUN

_____ PLURAL NOUN

_____ ADJECTIVE

_____ NOUN

_____ PART OF THE BODY (PLURAL)

_____ PERSON IN ROOM

_____ PART OF THE BODY

MAD LIBS®
FIELD TRIP TO THE ZOO

Okay, class! Here we are at the _____ zoo. It is a/an
                                    ADJECTIVE

_____ place to enjoy _____ experiences, but in
      ADJECTIVE   ADJECTIVE

order to do so, you must obey these _____ rules.
                                          ADJECTIVE

Rule #1 is personal: Have a/an _____ time.
                                      ADJECTIVE

Rule #2: Please don't feed the _____. They eat scientifically
                                    PLURAL NOUN

formulated _____ to ensure they remain in _____
              PLURAL NOUN   ADJECTIVE

health. Human food can upset their _____ and make them
                                    PART OF THE BODY (PLURAL)

sicker than a/an _____.
                      NOUN

Rule #3: Don't litter. Make sure you throw all of your _____
                                                              ADJECTIVE

wrappers and plastic _____ into trash _____ to
                          PLURAL NOUN   PLURAL NOUN

keep the zoo sparkling and _____.
                                ADJECTIVE

Rule #4: Respect boundaries. When you approach a wild _____
                                                              NOUN

cage, keep your _____ to yourself at all times. Last year,
                PART OF THE BODY (PLURAL)

_____ attempted to pet an orangutan and almost lost his/her
   PERSON IN ROOM

left _____.
      PART OF THE BODY

From MAD ABOUT ANIMALS MAD LIBS® • Copyright © 2009 by Price Stern Sloan,
an imprint of Penguin Group (USA) Inc., 345 Hudson Street, New York, NY 10014.

MAD LIBS® is fun to play with friends, but you can also play it by yourself! To begin with, DO NOT look at the story on the page below. Fill in the blanks on this page with the words called for. Then, using the words you have selected, fill in the blank spaces in the story.

Now you've created your own hilarious MAD LIBS® game!

LEGENDARY CREATURES

ADJECTIVE _____

ADJECTIVE _____

PLURAL NOUN _____

NOUN _____

ADJECTIVE _____

PLURAL NOUN _____

A PLACE _____

ADJECTIVE _____

NOUN _____

PART OF THE BODY _____

NOUN _____

ADJECTIVE _____

ADJECTIVE _____

NOUN _____

PLURAL NOUN _____

PLURAL NOUN _____

ADJECTIVE _____

MAD LIBS
LEGENDARY CREATURES

Throughout time, man has heard _____ tales of
ADJECTIVE

_____, mythical creatures that challenge the imagination.
ADJECTIVE

Here are the most famous of these _____:
PLURAL NOUN

- The **mermaid**, half human, half _____, was known to sing
NOUN

  _____ songs that caused sailors to crash their
ADJECTIVE

  _____ in the middle of (the) _____.
PLURAL NOUN   A PLACE

- The **unicorn** was described as a/an _____ horse
ADJECTIVE

  with a pointy _____ in the middle of its _____,
NOUN   PART OF THE BODY

  a billy-goat beard, a lion's _____, and _____
NOUN   ADJECTIVE

  hooves. It was believed to bring _____ luck to those who
ADJECTIVE

  were fortunate enough to see it.

- The **griffin** had the body of a/an _____ and the head and
NOUN

  _____ of an eagle. Legend has it that they guarded treasures of
PLURAL NOUN

  priceless _____. It is also believed they had the power to
PLURAL NOUN

  make a/an _____ man see.
ADJECTIVE

From MAD ABOUT ANIMALS MAD LIBS® • Copyright © 2009 by Price Stern Sloan,
an imprint of Penguin Group (USA) Inc., 345 Hudson Street, New York, NY 10014.

MAD LIBS® is fun to play with friends, but you can also play it by yourself! To begin with, DO NOT look at the story on the page below. Fill in the blanks on this page with the words called for. Then, using the words you have selected, fill in the blank spaces in the story.

Now you've created your own hilarious MAD LIBS® game!

CATS VS. DOGS, PART 1

ADJECTIVE _____

ADJECTIVE _____

VERB _____

NOUN _____

PLURAL NOUN _____

NOUN _____

PART OF THE BODY (PLURAL) _____

NOUN _____

ADJECTIVE _____

PART OF THE BODY _____

ADJECTIVE _____

PART OF THE BODY _____

NUMBER _____

MAD LIBS®
CATS VS. DOGS, PART 1

The _____ debate remains: Which pet is better, a cat or a dog?
            ADJECTIVE

Here are some *purr*-fect reasons why cats make _____ pets:
                                                      ADJECTIVE

• Cats come and _____ as they please, exploring the neighbor's
                      VERB

    _____, climbing tall _____, or basking in the
          NOUN   PLURAL NOUN

    midday _____.
                NOUN

• Cats are mysterious. Take one look into a cat's diamond-shaped

    _____, and you're sure it's reading your _____.
    PART OF THE BODY (PLURAL)   NOUN

• Cats are known for their _____ cleanliness. They wash
                                  ADJECTIVE

    themselves by licking their fur with their scratchy _____.
                                                              PART OF THE BODY

• Cats purr. It's a truly _____ sound that can even win the
                              ADJECTIVE

    _____ of a non–cat lover.
    PART OF THE BODY

• Finally, a cat is reputed to have _____ lives, which makes
                                          NUMBER

    it the cat's meow!

CATS VS. DOGS, PART 2

_____ ADJECTIVE

_____ NOUN

_____ ADJECTIVE

_____ NOUN

_____ ADVERB

_____ PART OF THE BODY

_____ NUMBER

_____ NOUN

_____ ADJECTIVE

_____ ADJECTIVE

_____ NUMBER

_____ ADJECTIVE

_____ ADJECTIVE

_____ ADJECTIVE

_____ NOUN

_____ NOUN

_____ NOUN

_____ NOUN

MAD LIBS®
CATS VS. DOGS, PART 2

Now, from the opposing side—here are a few _____ reasons
                                              ADJECTIVE

why dogs are considered man's best _____ :
                                          NOUN

• Dogs are _____ companions. They love to play. You can throw
              ADJECTIVE

  a rubber _____ and a dog will _____ chase it and
            NOUN   ADVERB

  carry it back to you in its _____ at least _____ times.
                              PART OF THE BODY   NUMBER

• Dogs can keep your _____ safe. Their _____ sense
                      NOUN   ADJECTIVE

  of hearing and _____ sense of smell justify the term *watchdog*.
                  ADJECTIVE

• There are more than _____ breeds of dogs. You can pick a/an
                        NUMBER

  _____ Chihuahua or a/an _____ Dane, and each
    ADJECTIVE   ADJECTIVE

  will have its own _____ personality.
                    ADJECTIVE

• You can't get a more loyal _____ than a dog. Just rub a dog's
                              NOUN

  _____ and you will have a/an _____ for life.
    NOUN   NOUN

• And the good news—a dog's bark is usually worse than its _____ !
                                                            NOUN

MAD LIBS® is fun to play with friends, but you can also play it by yourself! To begin with, DO NOT look at the story on the page below. Fill in the blanks on this page with the words called for. Then, using the words you have selected, fill in the blank spaces in the story.

Now you've created your own hilarious MAD LIBS® game!

DINO-MITE

ADJECTIVE _____

VERB (PAST TENSE) _____

PERSON IN ROOM _____

ADJECTIVE _____

PART OF THE BODY _____

PLURAL NOUN _____

NOUN _____

PLURAL NOUN _____

ADJECTIVE _____

ADJECTIVE _____

NOUN _____

ADJECTIVE _____

ADJECTIVE _____

PLURAL NOUN _____

NOUN _____

ADJECTIVE _____

TYPE OF LIQUID _____

PLURAL NOUN _____

PLURAL NOUN _____

NOUN _____

MAD LIBS®
DINO-MITE

Millions of years ago, _____ creatures called dinosaurs
                          ADJECTIVE

_____ all over the earth. The largest was the Tyrannosaurus
VERB (PAST TENSE)

_____. Strangely, this _____ beast had a small
PERSON IN ROOM   ADJECTIVE

_____ and was a scavenger that ate mostly _____.
PART OF THE BODY   PLURAL NOUN

The brontosaurus, an herbivore, had a very long _____,
                                                  NOUN

which helped it reach up and eat _____ from the tops of
                                  PLURAL NOUN

_____ trees. The stegosaurus had _____ scales that
ADJECTIVE   ADJECTIVE

were used as armor when it was attacked by a/an _____, and
                                                 NOUN

it ate a variety of _____ fruits and _____ foliage.
                     ADJECTIVE   ADJECTIVE

Unfortunately, dinosaurs disappeared long before human _____
                                                        PLURAL NOUN

appeared on earth. What happened to them? Scientists think a giant

_____ fell from space, creating a/an _____
NOUN   ADJECTIVE

wave of _____ and dust that destroyed these magnificent
         TYPE OF LIQUID

_____. Today, archeologists are still digging up dinosaur
PLURAL NOUN

_____, which can be seen in museums all over the
PLURAL NOUN

_____.
NOUN

MAD LIBS® is fun to play with friends, but you can also play it by yourself! To begin with, DO NOT look at the story on the page below. Fill in the blanks on this page with the words called for. Then, using the words you have selected, fill in the blank spaces in the story.

Now you've created your own hilarious MAD LIBS® game!

AMAZING DADS

ADJECTIVE _____

PLURAL NOUN _____

PLURAL NOUN _____

ADJECTIVE _____

ADJECTIVE _____

NUMBER _____

ADJECTIVE _____

PLURAL NOUN _____

NOUN _____

PART OF THE BODY _____

ADJECTIVE _____

PLURAL NOUN _____

NOUN _____

ADJECTIVE _____

ADJECTIVE _____

PART OF THE BODY _____

NUMBER _____

ADJECTIVE _____

NOUN _____

MAD LIBS®
AMAZING DADS

You hear a lot about _____ mothers in the wild, nurturing
                         ADJECTIVE

and taking care of their _____. But what most
                              PLURAL NOUN

_____ don't know is that there are a lot of great animal
    PLURAL NOUN

dads, too. A/An _____ example is the _____
                    ADJECTIVE   ADJECTIVE

sea horse. After a courtship dance of _____ hours, the female
                                           NUMBER

gives her _____ eggs to the male, who carries them until they
              ADJECTIVE

hatch. Emperor penguins are hands-on _____, too. After
                                          PLURAL NOUN

the mother lays a/an _____ , the dad carries it in his
                          NOUN

_____ to keep it _____ and warm while she
    PART OF THE BODY   ADJECTIVE

goes off to look for _____ to eat. He holds on to the
                          PLURAL NOUN

_____ throughout the cold, _____ winter.
    NOUN   ADJECTIVE

Another example of dad care is the _____ cardinal fish.
                                         ADJECTIVE

After the female fertilizes the eggs, the proud father keeps them in his

_____ for _____ days, until they hatch.
    PART OF THE BODY   NUMBER

Each of these _____ fathers deserves a trophy that says
                   ADJECTIVE

"World's #1 _____!"
                NOUN

From MAD ABOUT ANIMALS MAD LIBS® • Copyright © 2009 by Price Stern Sloan,
an imprint of Penguin Group (USA) Inc., 345 Hudson Street, New York, NY 10014.

MAD LIBS® is fun to play with friends, but you can also play it by yourself! To begin with, DO NOT look at the story on the page below. Fill in the blanks on this page with the words called for. Then, using the words you have selected, fill in the blank spaces in the story.

Now you've created your own hilarious MAD LIBS® game!

PANDAMANIA

_____ PLURAL NOUN

_____ ADJECTIVE

_____ NOUN

_____ ADJECTIVE

_____ NOUN

_____ VERB ENDING IN "ING"

_____ PLURAL NOUN

_____ EXCLAMATION

_____ PART OF THE BODY (PLURAL)

_____ ADJECTIVE

_____ PART OF THE BODY (PLURAL)

_____ NOUN

_____ NOUN

_____ NOUN

_____ PLURAL NOUN

_____ PLURAL NOUN

MAD LIBS
PANDAMANIA

Welcome back to the *World of Wild* _____. When we left off,

PLURAL NOUN

we were tracking the _____ panda in the forests of China,

ADJECTIVE

hoping to catch a glimpse of a newborn _____. Now, we are

NOUN

making our way through the _____ bamboo forest, trying

ADJECTIVE

to be as quiet as a/an _____. Wait! Something is

NOUN

_____ behind a bush! We can't see it, so we have to part some

VERB ENDING IN "ING"

thick bamboo _____. _____! I can't believe

PLURAL NOUN   EXCLAMATION

my _____. There is a mother panda, cradling her

PART OF THE BODY (PLURAL)

_____ cub in her _____. The baby

ADJECTIVE   PART OF THE BODY (PLURAL)

is the size of a miniature _____! It's the most beautiful

NOUN

_____ I've ever seen. Uh-oh, the mother _____

NOUN   NOUN

doesn't look too happy that we're here. Oh my _____, it

PLURAL NOUN

looks like she's coming after us! Run for your _____!

PLURAL NOUN

DOLPHINSPEAK

ADJECTIVE _____

PLURAL NOUN _____

NOUN _____

ADJECTIVE _____

PLURAL NOUN _____

ADJECTIVE _____

ADJECTIVE _____

PLURAL NOUN _____

ADJECTIVE _____

PLURAL NOUN _____

PART OF THE BODY (PLURAL) _____

OCCUPATION _____

ADJECTIVE _____

PERSON IN ROOM _____

ADVERB _____

MAD LIBS® is fun to play with friends, but you can also play it by yourself! To begin with, DO NOT look at the story on the page below. Fill in the blanks on this page with the words called for. Then, using the words you have selected, fill in the blank spaces in the story.

Now you've created your own hilarious MAD LIBS® game!

MAD LIBS
DOLPHINSPEAK

Humans have many _____ ways of communicating with
                        ADJECTIVE

one another. Today we depend on TV, cell _____, and
                                              PLURAL NOUN

e-_____ to get our information. Dolphins may not use
        NOUN

technology as _____ as ours, but they are highly advanced
                  ADJECTIVE

_____ with a/an _____ capacity for language
    PLURAL NOUN   ADJECTIVE

skills. They communicate by making _____ noises that sound
                                          ADJECTIVE

like _____, called sonar. Their _____ sounds bounce
        PLURAL NOUN   ADJECTIVE

off underwater _____, traveling to the _____
                    PLURAL NOUN   PART OF THE BODY (PLURAL)

of other dolphins. This makes it easy for dolphins to alert their friends that

there's a deep-sea _____ swimming nearby, or to share the latest
                        OCCUPATION

_____ gossip about _____. So the next time
    ADJECTIVE   PERSON IN ROOM

you're at an aquarium, listen _____ to the dolphins: They
                                    ADVERB

might just be talking about you!

MAD LIBS® is fun to play with friends, but you can also play it by yourself! To begin with, DO NOT look at the story on the page below. Fill in the blanks on this page with the words called for. Then, using the words you have selected, fill in the blank spaces in the story.

Now you've created your own hilarious MAD LIBS® game!

IN THE NURSERY, PART 1

_____ NOUN

_____ NOUN

_____ ADJECTIVE

_____ ADVERB

_____ PLURAL NOUN

_____ PLURAL NOUN

_____ PLURAL NOUN

_____ NOUN

_____ ADJECTIVE

_____ NUMBER

_____ NOUN

_____ PLURAL NOUN

_____ ADJECTIVE

_____ VERB ENDING IN "ING"

_____ PLURAL NOUN

_____ ADJECTIVE

_____ ADJECTIVE

_____ ADJECTIVE

_____ ADJECTIVE

MAD LIBS®
IN THE NURSERY, PART 1

Most _____ bedtime stories revolve around _____
         ADJECTIVE   ADJECTIVE

animals—and they usually end happily. Here are some _____
                                                              ADJECTIVE

examples of this theory:

- "The Three _____ Pigs": The pigs build houses made of straw,
                ADJECTIVE

  sticks, and _____. By huffing and _____, the big,
               PLURAL NOUN   VERB ENDING IN "ING"

  _____ wolf blows the first two _____ down—
        ADJECTIVE   PLURAL NOUN

  but he just can't blow down the brick _____.
                                              NOUN

- "Goldilocks and the _____ Bears": While the
                              NUMBER

  _____ bears are away, Goldilocks sneaks in their house,
        ADJECTIVE

  eats their _____ , sits in their _____, and sleeps
                 NOUN   PLURAL NOUN

  in their _____. The three _____ come
              PLURAL NOUN   PLURAL NOUN

  home, but Goldilocks _____ escapes.
                              ADVERB

- "The Frog Prince": A/An _____ princess befriends a frog,
                                 ADJECTIVE

  but when she kisses his _____ , he transforms into a
                                 NOUN

  handsome _____.
                NOUN

MAD LIBS® is fun to play with friends, but you can also play it by yourself! To begin with, DO NOT look at the story on the page below. Fill in the blanks on this page with the words called for. Then, using the words you have selected, fill in the blank spaces in the story.

Now you've created your own hilarious MAD LIBS® game!

IN THE NURSERY, PART 2

_____ ADJECTIVE

_____ ADJECTIVE

_____ PLURAL NOUN

_____ NOUN

_____ PLURAL NOUN

_____ ADJECTIVE

_____ PLURAL NOUN

_____ PART OF THE BODY (PLURAL)

_____ ADJECTIVE

_____ ADJECTIVE

_____ ADJECTIVE

_____ ADJECTIVE

_____ NOUN

_____ ADJECTIVE

_____ VERB

_____ PLURAL NOUN

_____ NOUN

_____ NOUN

- "Little Red Riding _____": This story features another big,
NOUN

bad _____. This wolf disguises himself as Little Red's
NOUN

grandmother. "My, what big _____ you have!" she cries.
PLURAL NOUN

"The better to _____ you with, my dear," the wolf replies.
VERB

Ultimately, Little Red _____ Hood is rescued by a/an
ADJECTIVE

_____.
NOUN

- "The _____ Duckling": The duckling feels he's more
ADJECTIVE

_____ than the other ducks. All his friends taunt him:
ADJECTIVE

"Look how _____ he is! He's not one of us!" When he
ADJECTIVE

turns into a/an _____ swan, they can't believe their
ADJECTIVE

_____.
PART OF THE BODY (PLURAL)

- "Puss in _____": A/An _____ miller's son inherits
PLURAL NOUN   ADJECTIVE

a cat who promises him riches and _____ in return for a
PLURAL NOUN

bag containing a/an _____ and a pair of high leather
NOUN

_____. Eventually the _____ son marries
PLURAL NOUN   ADJECTIVE

a/an _____ princess.
ADJECTIVE

MAD LIBS® is fun to play with friends, but you can also play it by yourself! To begin with, DO NOT look at the story on the page below. Fill in the blanks on this page with the words called for. Then, using the words you have selected, fill in the blank spaces in the story.

Now you've created your own hilarious MAD LIBS® game!

FIRST PETS

COLOR _____

ADJECTIVE _____

NOUN _____

ADJECTIVE _____

NOUN _____

PLURAL NOUN _____

NOUN _____

NOUN _____

SILLY WORD _____

PERSON IN ROOM _____

ADJECTIVE _____

PERSON IN ROOM _____

PERSON IN ROOM _____

ADJECTIVE _____

NOUN _____

ADJECTIVE _____

ADJECTIVE _____

VERB _____

ADJECTIVE _____

MAD LIBS
FIRST PETS

When an American president gets elected, the entire family moves into

the _____ House—including their _____
        COLOR   ADJECTIVE

pets. Our first _____, George Washington, had seven
                    NOUN

_____ hounds, horses, and even a parrot that said, "Polly want
    ADJECTIVE

a/an _____." John Quincy Adams owned silkworms that made
        NOUN

_____ for his wife. Zachary Taylor kept a horse on the front lawn
  PLURAL NOUN

of the White _____. Calvin Coolidge owned enough
                    NOUN

animals for a zoo, including a pygmy _____, a pair of
                                            NOUN

birds named _____ and _____, and
                SILLY WORD   PERSON IN ROOM

even a/an _____ wallaby. John F. Kennedy had two hamsters
            ADJECTIVE

named _____ and _____. More recently,
        PERSON IN ROOM   PERSON IN ROOM

President Clinton had a/an _____ cat named Socks, who didn't
                            ADJECTIVE

get along with their Labrador _____ named Buddy. So now you
                                NOUN

know how _____ politicians learned to _____
            ADJECTIVE   VERB

like cats and dogs—from their _____ pets!
                                ADJECTIVE

From MAD ABOUT ANIMALS MAD LIBS® • Copyright © 2009 by Price Stern Sloan,
an imprint of Penguin Group (USA) Inc., 345 Hudson Street, New York, NY 10014.

MAD LIBS® is fun to play with friends, but you can also play it by yourself! To begin with, DO NOT look at the story on the page below. Fill in the blanks on this page with the words called for. Then, using the words you have selected, fill in the blank spaces in the story.

Now you've created your own hilarious MAD LIBS® game!

THE KING OF BUTTERFLIES

PLURAL NOUN _____

ADJECTIVE _____

NOUN _____

ADJECTIVE _____

ADJECTIVE _____

NUMBER _____

ADJECTIVE _____

PLURAL NOUN _____

PLURAL NOUN _____

ADJECTIVE _____

ADJECTIVE _____

PLURAL NOUN _____

ADJECTIVE _____

PART OF THE BODY (PLURAL) _____

MAD LIBS

THE KING OF BUTTERFLIES

The monarch butterfly, with its distinctive black and yellow

_____ , is one of the most _____ insects on the
    PLURAL NOUN   ADJECTIVE

planet. But it doesn't start life as a beautiful _____. A
                                 NOUN

monarch egg first hatches into a/an _____ caterpillar that spins
                         ADJECTIVE

a/an _____ covering made of silk called a cocoon. Over a period
    ADJECTIVE

of _____ weeks, the caterpillar turns into a/an _____
    NUMBER   ADJECTIVE

butterfly. When the monarch is able to spread its _____, it flies
                               PLURAL NOUN

away to feed on a variety of _____, including milkweed, red
                         PLURAL NOUN

clover, and other _____ flowers. Monarchs are especially noted
               ADJECTIVE

for their _____ migrations across the country and, upon
        ADJECTIVE

occasion, across the Atlantic and Pacific _____. In flight, these
                      PLURAL NOUN

_____ butterflies are a sight for sore _____!
    ADJECTIVE   PART OF THE BODY (PLURAL)

From MAD ABOUT ANIMALS MAD LIBS® • Copyright © 2009 by Price Stern Sloan,
an imprint of Penguin Group (USA) Inc., 345 Hudson Street, New York, NY 10014.

MAD LIBS® is fun to play with friends, but you can also play it by yourself! To begin with, DO NOT look at the story on the page below. Fill in the blanks on this page with the words called for. Then, using the words you have selected, fill in the blank spaces in the story.

Now you've created your own hilarious MAD LIBS® game!

SNAKE SCARE

PLURAL NOUN _____

SILLY WORD _____

PLURAL NOUN _____

ADJECTIVE _____

PART OF THE BODY _____

VERB ENDING IN "ING" _____

ADJECTIVE _____

ADJECTIVE _____

NOUN _____

PART OF THE BODY _____

VERB (PAST TENSE) _____

NOUN _____

PART OF THE BODY (PLURAL) _____

ADJECTIVE _____

NOUN _____

NOUN _____

PART OF THE BODY _____

VERB _____

MAD LIBS®
SNAKE SCARE

In my opinion, snakes are the scariest _____ on the planet. My
PLURAL NOUN

fear of snakes began when I was away at Camp _____ one
SILLY WORD

summer. We were seated around a campfire roasting _____
PLURAL NOUN

on sticks when I became very tired and decided to go back to my

_____ cabin to catch some shut-_____. I was snug in
ADJECTIVE   PART OF THE BODY

my _____ bag when I suddenly felt something _____
VERB ENDING IN "ING"   ADJECTIVE

touching my leg. At first I thought it was a/an _____ dream,
ADJECTIVE

but then I heard a hissing like a boiling tea _____, and felt
NOUN

something slithering up my _____! I _____ at the
PART OF THE BODY   VERB (PAST TENSE)

top of my lungs and was out of my _____ in a split second. I
NOUN

ran as fast as my _____ could carry me and dove into the
PART OF THE BODY (PLURAL)

_____ pond, hoping to ditch the snake. To my embarrassment,
ADJECTIVE

it turned out to be a harmless garter _____. But today, just the
NOUN

thought of a snake's scaly _____ and rattling _____
NOUN   PART OF THE BODY

makes my skin _____!
VERB

MAD LIBS® is fun to play with friends, but you can also play it by yourself! To begin with, DO NOT look at the story on the page below. Fill in the blanks on this page with the words called for. Then, using the words you have selected, fill in the blank spaces in the story.

Now you've created your own hilarious MAD LIBS® game!

FELINE PHARAOHS

ADJECTIVE _____

ADJECTIVE _____

PLURAL NOUN _____

NOUN _____

ADJECTIVE _____

PLURAL NOUN _____

ADJECTIVE _____

NOUN _____

VERB ENDING IN "ING" _____

ADJECTIVE _____

PART OF THE BODY _____

PLURAL NOUN _____

ADJECTIVE _____

ADJECTIVE _____

NOUN _____

PLURAL NOUN _____

NOUN _____

MAD LIBS®
FELINE PHARAOHS

In the ancient land of _____ mummies and _____
                         ADJECTIVE   ADJECTIVE

pyramids, it was great to be a cat. All of today's cats are descended from

those ancient _____ of Egypt. Beginning as a wild and
                    PLURAL NOUN

_____ species, the cat was quickly domesticated and became a
   ADJECTIVE

symbol of grace and _____. Kings, queens, and even common
                            NOUN

_____ discovered that cats made _____
    PLURAL NOUN   ADJECTIVE

companions. Before long, felines became revered in Egyptian society. Every

Egyptian _____ believed that if you saw a cat while you were
               NOUN

_____ seeds, you would have a/an _____
VERB ENDING IN "ING"   ADJECTIVE

harvest. Images of cats were seen on everything from jewelry for the

_____ to cat-shaped _____ that women wore in
PART OF THE BODY   PLURAL NOUN

their _____ hair. Many homes had _____
          ADJECTIVE   ADJECTIVE

14-karat _____ cat statues. Egyptians even mummified cats, so
              NOUN

that their owners could spend the afterlife with their beloved

_____! Isn't that the _____'s meow?
   PLURAL NOUN   NOUN

DOWN ON THE FARM

PERSON IN ROOM (FEMALE) _____

ADJECTIVE _____

VERB ENDING IN "ING" _____

NOUN _____

PLURAL NOUN _____

NOUN _____

ADJECTIVE _____

PLURAL NOUN _____

PLURAL NOUN _____

ADJECTIVE _____

ADJECTIVE _____

PLURAL NOUN _____

PERSON IN ROOM _____

ADJECTIVE _____

PART OF THE BODY _____

NOUN _____

ADJECTIVE _____

My summer vacation on Aunt _____'s farm has
                                    PERSON IN ROOM (FEMALE)

been fun, but it's also been a lot of _____ work. This morning,
                                         ADJECTIVE

as usual, I woke up as the rooster was _____, and ate a hearty
                                          VERB ENDING IN "ING"

_____ of _____ and syrup, with eggs freshly laid
      NOUN   PLURAL NOUN

by the farm _____. Then, I went out to the _____
                 NOUN   ADJECTIVE

barn to do my chores. I fed and groomed the horses, brushing their

_____ and cleaning their _____. I also cleaned
   PLURAL NOUN   PLURAL NOUN

their _____ trough, which smelled like _____
         ADJECTIVE   ADJECTIVE

_____. Finally, I milked _____, the cow. I sat on
   PLURAL NOUN   PERSON IN ROOM

a/an _____ stool beneath the cow's _____, and
        ADJECTIVE   PART OF THE BODY

filled an entire _____ full of fresh milk. Yup, just another
                      NOUN

_____ day down on the farm!
   ADJECTIVE

MAD LIBS® is fun to play with friends, but you can also play it by yourself! To begin with, DO NOT look at the story on the page below. Fill in the blanks on this page with the words called for. Then, using the words you have selected, fill in the blank spaces in the story.

Now you've created your own hilarious MAD LIBS® game!

QUEEN BEE

_____ PLURAL NOUN

_____ ADJECTIVE

_____ NOUN

_____ VERB

_____ ADJECTIVE

_____ ADJECTIVE

_____ NOUN

_____ ADJECTIVE

_____ ADJECTIVE

_____ PLURAL NOUN

_____ TYPE OF LIQUID

_____ PLURAL NOUN

_____ NOUN

_____ PLURAL NOUN

_____ ADJECTIVE

_____ ADJECTIVE

MAD LIBS
QUEEN BEE

The following is an interview with a Bee Bee C bee reporter and a Queen

Bee, to be read aloud by two _____.
                                        PLURAL NOUN

Q: We are here with Her _____ Highness, the Queen
                                   ADJECTIVE

_____, who has agreed to _____ with us
          NOUN   VERB

today. Your Highness, describe your _____ hive.
                                               ADJECTIVE

A: I am proud to reign over forty thousand _____ bees who
                                                        ADJECTIVE

work around the _____. You know what they say, "As
                          NOUN

_____ as a bee!"
        ADJECTIVE

Q: What are some _____ bee facts that we may not know?
                          ADJECTIVE

A: Well, I lay over two thousand _____ a day. Other bees do
                                          PLURAL NOUN

everything from making sweet golden _____ to pollinating
                                              TYPE OF LIQUID

_____. And each bee has its own unique _____
     PLURAL NOUN   NOUN

so that I can tell them apart.

Q: Any other _____ of wisdom for this _____ reporter?
                   PLURAL NOUN   ADJECTIVE

A: Honey, _____ words may sting you, but just *bee* yourself.
                ADJECTIVE

From MAD ABOUT ANIMALS MAD LIBS® • Copyright © 2009 by Price Stern Sloan,
an imprint of Penguin Group (USA) Inc., 345 Hudson Street, New York, NY 10014.

MAD LIBS®

PEACE, LOVE, AND MAD LIBS

by Roger Price and Leonard Stern

PSS!

PRICE STERN SLOAN

An Imprint of Penguin Group (USA) Inc.

PRICE STERN SLOAN
Published by the Penguin Group
Penguin Group (USA) Inc., 375 Hudson Street, New York, New York 10014, USA
Penguin Group (Canada), 90 Eglinton Avenue East, Suite 700, Toronto, Ontario M4P 2Y3, Canada
(a division of Pearson Penguin Canada Inc.)
Penguin Books Ltd, 80 Strand, London WC2R 0RL, England
Penguin Ireland, 25 St Stephen's Green, Dublin 2, Ireland (a division of Penguin Books Ltd)
Penguin Group (Australia), 707 Collins Street, Melbourne, Victoria 3008, Australia
(a division of Pearson Australia Group Pty Ltd)
Penguin Books India Pvt Ltd, 11 Community Centre, Panchsheel Park, New Delhi—110 017, India
Penguin Group (NZ), 67 Apollo Drive, Rosedale, Auckland 0632, New Zealand
(a division of Pearson New Zealand Ltd)
Penguin Books (South Africa), Rosebank Office Park, 181 Jan Smuts Avenue,
Parktown North 2193, South Africa
Penguin China, B7 Jiaming Center, 27 East Third Ring Road North,
Chaoyang District, Beijing 100020, China

Penguin Books Ltd, Registered Offices: 80 Strand, London WC2R 0RL, England

Mad About Mad Libs published in 2013 by Price Stern Sloan,
a division of Penguin Young Readers Group, 345 Hudson Street, New York, New York 10014.

ALWAYS LEARNING   **PEARSON**

INSTRUCTIONS

MAD LIBS® is a game for people who don't like games!
It can be played by one, two, three, four, or forty.

• RIDICULOUSLY SIMPLE DIRECTIONS

In this tablet you will find stories containing blank spaces where words are left out. One player, the **READER**, selects one of these stories. The **READER** does not tell anyone what the story is about. Instead, he/she asks the other players, the **WRITERS**, to give him/her words. These words are used to fill in the blank spaces in the story.

• TO PLAY

The **READER** asks each **WRITER** in turn to call out a word—an adjective or a noun or whatever the space calls for—and uses them to fill in the blank spaces in the story. The result is a **MAD LIBS®** game.

When the **READER** then reads the completed **MAD LIBS®** game to the other players, they will discover that they have written a story that is fantastic, screamingly funny, shocking, silly, crazy, or just plain dumb—depending upon which words each **WRITER** called out.

• EXAMPLE (*Before* and *After*)

"_____!" he said _____
     EXCLAMATION   ADVERB

as he jumped into his convertible _____ and
                                              NOUN

drove off with his _____ wife.
                          ADJECTIVE

"_____*Ouch*_____!" he said _____*stupidly*_____
     EXCLAMATION   ADVERB

as he jumped into his convertible _____*cat*_____ and
                                              NOUN

drove off with his _____*brave*_____ wife.
                          ADJECTIVE

MAD LIBS®

QUICK REVIEW

In case you have forgotten what adjectives, adverbs, nouns, and verbs are, here is a quick review:

An **ADJECTIVE** describes something or somebody. *Lumpy, soft, ugly, messy,* and *short* are adjectives.

An **ADVERB** tells how something is done. It modifies a verb and usually ends in "ly." *Modestly, stupidly, greedily,* and *carefully* are adverbs.

A **NOUN** is the name of a person, place, or thing. *Sidewalk, umbrella, bridle, bathtub,* and *nose* are nouns.

A **VERB** is an action word. *Run, pitch, jump,* and *swim* are verbs. Put the verbs in past tense if the directions say PAST TENSE. *Ran, pitched, jumped,* and *swam* are verbs in the past tense.

When we ask for **A PLACE**, we mean any sort of place: a country or city *(Spain, Cleveland)* or a room *(bathroom, kitchen).*

An **EXCLAMATION** or **SILLY WORD** is any sort of funny sound, gasp, grunt, or outcry, like *Wow!, Ouch!, Whomp!, Ick!,* and *Gadzooks!*

When we ask for specific words, like a **NUMBER**, a **COLOR**, an **ANIMAL**, or a **PART OF THE BODY**, we mean a word that is one of those things, like *seven, blue, horse,* or *head.*

When we ask for a **PLURAL**, it means more than one. For example, *cat* pluralized is *cats.*

MAD LIBS® is fun to play with friends, but you can also play it by yourself! To begin with, DO NOT look at the story on the page below. Fill in the blanks on this page with the words called for. Then, using the words you have selected, fill in the blank spaces in the story.

Now you've created your own hilarious MAD LIBS® game!

PEACE IS THE WORD

NOUN _____

NUMBER _____

PLURAL NOUN _____

COLOR _____

NOUN _____

NOUN _____

NOUN _____

PERSON IN ROOM _____

VERB (PAST TENSE) _____

NOUN _____

ADJECTIVE _____

PART OF THE BODY (PLURAL) _____

ADJECTIVE _____

NOUN _____

PLURAL NOUN _____

PLURAL NOUN _____

MAD LIBS®
PEACE IS THE WORD

Our _____ Studies teacher had us write a/an _____-
         NOUN   NUMBER

word paper on the different symbols for peace. I learned many interesting

_____ , such as:
   PLURAL NOUN

• The _____ dove is a symbol of love, peace, and _____ .
         COLOR   NOUN

• The olive _____ represents a peace offering or goodwill
                 NOUN

gesture, as in: *The next-door neighbors extended a/an* _____
                                                              NOUN

branch to _____ *after their dog* _____ *on his/*
              PERSON IN ROOM   VERB (PAST TENSE)

her _____ .
         NOUN

• The "V" sign is a/an _____ gesture made by holding up two
                          ADJECTIVE

_____ in the shape of the letter *V.*
PART OF THE BODY (PLURAL)

• The peace sign is one of the most _____ symbols in the
                                       ADJECTIVE

_____ . It was popular with hippies, who spray-painted it
   NOUN

on _____ while shouting, "Give _____ a chance!"
     PLURAL NOUN   PLURAL NOUN

MAD LIBS® is fun to play with friends, but you can also play it by yourself! To begin with, DO NOT look at the story on the page below. Fill in the blanks on this page with the words called for. Then, using the words you have selected, fill in the blank spaces in the story.

Now you've created your own hilarious MAD LIBS® game!

THE HIPPIE SHACK

PART OF THE BODY _____

ADJECTIVE _____

NOUN _____

PLURAL NOUN _____

PLURAL NOUN _____

NOUN _____

ARTICLE OF CLOTHING _____

NOUN _____

PART OF THE BODY _____

ADJECTIVE _____

ADJECTIVE _____

NOUN _____

PLURAL NOUN _____

PART OF THE BODY _____

VERB ENDING IN "ING" _____

NOUN _____

ADJECTIVE _____

MAD LIBS®
THE HIPPIE SHACK

Are you a hippie wannabe? If so, visit the Hippie Shack. They'll outfit you

from head to _____ in the colorful, _____ clothing
　　　　　　　　PART OF THE BODY　　　　　　　　ADJECTIVE

worn by those _____ -loving flower _____ of the
　　　　　　　　　NOUN　　　　　　　　　　　　PLURAL NOUN

'60s! We suggest starting with basic bell-bottom _____ ,
　　　　　　　　　　　　　　　　　　　　　　　PLURAL NOUN

preferably a vintage pair with _____ -shaped patches sewn over
　　　　　　　　　　　　　　　NOUN

the holes. Then select any _____ with fringe, tie-dye, or a
　　　　　　　　　　ARTICLE OF CLOTHING

psychedelic _____ pattern. You can accessorize to your
　　　　　　　NOUN

_____'s content! We have some _____ belts and
PART OF THE BODY　　　　　　　　　　　　ADJECTIVE

_____ jewelry with the peace _____ displayed.
ADJECTIVE　　　　　　　　　　　　　　　NOUN

Or you can wear strings of beaded _____ , and we have scarves
　　　　　　　　　　　　　　　PLURAL NOUN

that wrap around your _____ . Trust us, when you step out of
　　　　　　　　　　PART OF THE BODY

the _____ room in your cool new threads, you'll not only look
　VERB ENDING IN "ING"

like a groovy _____ , you'll feel pretty _____ , too!
　　　　　NOUN　　　　　　　　　　　　ADJECTIVE

MAD LIBS® is fun to play with friends, but you can also play it by yourself! To begin with, DO NOT look at the story on the page below. Fill in the blanks on this page with the words called for. Then, using the words you have selected, fill in the blank spaces in the story.

Now you've created your own hilarious MAD LIBS® game!

HAPPENING

VERB _____

NUMBER _____

ADJECTIVE _____

ADJECTIVE _____

NOUN _____

ADJECTIVE _____

PLURAL NOUN _____

A PLACE _____

ADJECTIVE _____

PLURAL NOUN _____

PERSON IN ROOM _____

ANIMAL (PLURAL) _____

VERB ENDING IN "ING" _____

TYPE OF FOOD (PLURAL) _____

NOUN _____

ADJECTIVE _____

NOUN _____

VERB _____

NOUN _____

MAD LIBS

HAPPENING

Run, don't _____, to join _____ of your closest
          VERB   NUMBER

friends at the greatest _____ outdoor musical experience of our
                            ADJECTIVE

_____ generation. This once-in-a/an-_____
  ADJECTIVE   NOUN

event is guaranteed to provide a/an _____ weekend filled with
                                ADJECTIVE

music, peace, love, and _____ in the picturesque setting
                          PLURAL NOUN

of (the) _____ . Bands such as the _____
          A PLACE   ADJECTIVE

_____, _____ and the _____, the
  PLURAL NOUN   PERSON IN ROOM   ANIMAL (PLURAL)

_____ _____, and many more will be
  VERB ENDING IN "ING"   TYPE OF FOOD (PLURAL)

rocking the _____ all night long! This _____ happening
          NOUN   ADJECTIVE

will take place rain or _____, so _____ accordingly.
                 NOUN   VERB

It's sure to be a legendary _____!
                       NOUN

MAD LIBS® is fun to play with friends, but you can also play it by yourself! To begin with, DO NOT look at the story on the page below. Fill in the blanks on this page with the words called for. Then, using the words you have selected, fill in the blank spaces in the story.

Now you've created your own hilarious MAD LIBS® game!

WORLD PEACE...
AND OTHER PROMISES

ADJECTIVE _____

ADJECTIVE _____

PERSON IN ROOM _____

PLURAL NOUN _____

ADJECTIVE _____

ADVERB _____

ADJECTIVE _____

PLURAL NOUN _____

NOUN _____

PLURAL NOUN _____

TYPE OF LIQUID _____

NOUN _____

ADJECTIVE _____

ADVERB _____

PLURAL NOUN _____

PLURAL NOUN _____

PLURAL NOUN _____

NOUN _____

PERSON IN ROOM _____

ADJECTIVE _____

MAD LIBS
WORLD PEACE...
AND OTHER PROMISES

Our school is voting for this year's _____ president! Let's listen
                                        ADJECTIVE

in as the _____ candidate, _____ , makes his/her
            ADJECTIVE   PERSON IN ROOM

final campaign speech:

"My fellow _____: I know the _____ changes
              PLURAL NOUN   ADJECTIVE

you want and _____ deserve. If elected, I promise to put an
                  ADVERB

end to _____ homework and pop _____ . I will
          ADJECTIVE   PLURAL NOUN

expand the lunch menu to include _____-burgers and cheese-
                                    NOUN

stuffed _____ . I will fill every drinking fountain with chocolate
          PLURAL NOUN

_____ . I will see to it that the only acceptable exercise in gym
  TYPE OF LIQUID

class is dodge-_____ . Finally, for every _____
                  NOUN   ADJECTIVE

student in detention, I _____ swear to make video
                            ADVERB

_____ , comic _____ , and widescreen
  PLURAL NOUN   PLURAL NOUN

_____ available in the detention _____ . So
  PLURAL NOUN   NOUN

remember: A vote for _____ today is a vote for a/an
                        PERSON IN ROOM

_____ school tomorrow!"
  ADJECTIVE

MAD LIBS® is fun to play with friends, but you can also play it by yourself! To begin with, DO NOT look at the story on the page below. Fill in the blanks on this page with the words called for. Then, using the words you have selected, fill in the blank spaces in the story.

Now you've created your own hilarious MAD LIBS® game!

HAPPY CAMPERS

ADJECTIVE _____

ADJECTIVE _____

ADJECTIVE _____

PLURAL NOUN _____

PLURAL NOUN _____

ADJECTIVE _____

NOUN _____

VERB ENDING IN "ING" _____

NOUN _____

ARTICLE OF CLOTHING (PLURAL) _____

NOUN _____

PLURAL NOUN _____

TYPE OF LIQUID _____

VERB ENDING IN "ING" _____

ADJECTIVE _____

NOUN _____

MAD LIBS

HAPPY CAMPERS

When life gets too _____ , there's no better antidote than to
ADJECTIVE

forget the _____ grind and go camping with some
ADJECTIVE

_____ friends. With the moon and _____
ADJECTIVE   PLURAL NOUN

twinkling overhead and the sound of _____ chirping in the
PLURAL NOUN

woods, sitting around the campfire and singing a/an _____
ADJECTIVE

chorus or two of "She'll Be Coming 'Round the _____ " or
NOUN

"I've Been _____ on the Railroad" is a great way to restore
VERB ENDING IN "ING"

peace to your inner _____ . Or, if you choose, you can scare
NOUN

the _____ off everyone with _____
ARTICLE OF CLOTHING (PLURAL)   NOUN

stories. You can also just sit quietly, toasting _____ and
PLURAL NOUN

sipping mugs of steaming _____ before snuggling into
TYPE OF LIQUID

your _____ bag. Yes, there's nothing better than the
VERB ENDING IN "ING"

_____ outdoors to guarantee a good night's _____ !
ADJECTIVE   NOUN

From PEACE, LOVE, AND MAD LIBS® • Copyright © 2009 by Price Stern Sloan,
an imprint of Penguin Group (USA) Inc., 345 Hudson Street, New York, NY 10014.

FOR PEACE SAKE!

ADJECTIVE
_____

PLURAL NOUN
_____

VERB ENDING IN "ING"
_____

PART OF THE BODY (PLURAL)
_____

NOUN
_____

PLURAL NOUN
_____

ADVERB
_____

NOUN
_____

VERB
_____

PLURAL NOUN
_____

NUMBER
_____

PART OF THE BODY (PLURAL)
_____

PLURAL NOUN
_____

ADJECTIVE
_____

NOUN
_____

MAD LIBS® is fun to play with friends, but you can also play it by yourself! To begin with, DO NOT look at the story on the page below. Fill in the blanks on this page with the words called for. Then, using the words you have selected, fill in the blank spaces in the story.

Now you've created your own hilarious MAD LIBS® game!

MAD LIBS®
FOR PEACE SAKE!

My _____ brother and sister are at it again, fighting like cats
　　　ADJECTIVE

and _____. I've had enough. I've decided to give them a stern
　　　PLURAL NOUN

_____ to. I will look them straight in their _____
VERB ENDING IN "ING"　　　　　　　　　　　　　　　PART OF THE BODY (PLURAL)

and say, "Living under the same _____ means we're going to get on
　　　　　　　　　　　　　　　NOUN

one another's _____ from time to time, but you two are being
　　　　　　PLURAL NOUN

_____ insensitive! You don't have to argue at the drop of a/an
　　ADVERB

_____. Think before you _____. Take a few deep
　　NOUN　　　　　　　　　　　　　VERB

_____ and count to _____ . If you don't, I'm
　PLURAL NOUN　　　　　　　　　NUMBER

warning you, I'll take matters into my own _____
　　　　　　　　　　　　　　　PART OF THE BODY (PLURAL)

and knock you flat on your _____ ! Now let's have some
　　　　　　　　　　PLURAL NOUN

_____ peace and _____ ."
　ADJECTIVE　　　　　　　　NOUN

From PEACE, LOVE, AND MAD LIBS® • Copyright © 2009 by Price Stern Sloan,
an imprint of Penguin Group (USA) Inc., 345 Hudson Street, New York, NY 10014.

MAD LIBS® is fun to play with friends, but you can also play it by yourself! To begin with, DO NOT look at the story on the page below. Fill in the blanks on this page with the words called for. Then, using the words you have selected, fill in the blank spaces in the story.

Now you've created your own hilarious MAD LIBS® game!

FAR-OUT FOOD

ADJECTIVE _____

PART OF THE BODY _____

NOUN _____

NUMBER _____

ADJECTIVE _____

ADJECTIVE _____

NOUN _____

ADJECTIVE _____

PLURAL NOUN _____

ADJECTIVE _____

PLURAL NOUN _____

NOUN _____

ADVERB _____

NOUN _____

NOUN _____

PLURAL NOUN _____

PART OF THE BODY _____

ADJECTIVE _____

MAD LIBS®
FAR-OUT FOOD

Welcome to the Far-Out Café! Our _____ diner serves

<u>ADJECTIVE</u>

_____-lickin' good eats that are out of this _____ .

<u>PART OF THE BODY</u>   <u>NOUN</u>

Our most popular dishes are:

- **Hippie Hamburger**: _____ oz. of _____

      <u>NUMBER</u>   <u>ADJECTIVE</u>

beef on a/an _____ bun, stacked with sprouts, tomato, and

      <u>ADJECTIVE</u>

a/an _____ slice

      <u>NOUN</u>

- **Flower Child Chicken**: This _____ dish is served with

      <u>ADJECTIVE</u>

wild _____ and homegrown _____ vegetables

      <u>PLURAL NOUN</u>   <u>ADJECTIVE</u>

on a bed of flower _____

      <u>PLURAL NOUN</u>

- **Groovy Grilled Cheese**: Sharp _____ cheese melted between

      <u>NOUN</u>

two slices of _____ baked _____ , served with

      <u>ADVERB</u>   <u>NOUN</u>

_____ chips

      <u>NOUN</u>

- **Psychedelic Salad**: On a bed of dark leafy _____ , an array

      <u>PLURAL NOUN</u>

of creative exuberances that will tempt your _____ and

      <u>PART OF THE BODY</u>

provide a/an _____ meal in itself

      <u>ADJECTIVE</u>

MAD LIBS® is fun to play with friends, but you can also play it by yourself! To begin with, DO NOT look at the story on the page below. Fill in the blanks on this page with the words called for. Then, using the words you have selected, fill in the blank spaces in the story.

Now you've created your own hilarious MAD LIBS® game!

A LITTLE PEACE & QUIET

NOUN _____

NOUN _____

PLURAL NOUN _____

NOUN _____

NOUN _____

PLURAL NOUN _____

NOUN _____

ADVERB _____

PLURAL NOUN _____

PLURAL NOUN _____

PLURAL NOUN _____

PLURAL NOUN _____

PART OF THE BODY (PLURAL) _____

PLURAL NOUN _____

PLURAL NOUN _____

PLURAL NOUN _____

NOUN _____

MAD LIBS®
A LITTLE PEACE & QUIET

What would happen if you fell overboard from a/an _____
<u>NOUN</u>

and washed up on a deserted tropical _____ ? Here's a list
<u>NOUN</u>

of survival _____ :
<u>PLURAL NOUN</u>

• The human _____ requires one thing more than all
<u>NOUN</u>

others to survive: _____ . Without water, you would only last
<u>NOUN</u>

for a few _____ . So you'd have to find a source of fresh
<u>PLURAL NOUN</u>

running _____ and boil it before _____ drinking it.
<u>NOUN</u>   <u>ADVERB</u>

• Look for plants, _____ , and insects to eat. You can also
<u>PLURAL NOUN</u>

try leaves, berries, roots, and even the bark of some _____ .
<u>PLURAL NOUN</u>

• Food can also be hunted with primitive _____ . Use rocks,
<u>PLURAL NOUN</u>

sticks, ropes, _____ , or anything else you can get your
<u>PLURAL NOUN</u>

_____ on.
<u>PART OF THE BODY (PLURAL)</u>

• Gather _____ for a campfire. Rub two _____
<u>PLURAL NOUN</u>   <u>PLURAL NOUN</u>

together until a fire is created. You will have warmth and a way to

cook and boil your _____ . Perhaps most importantly,
<u>PLURAL NOUN</u>

you'll have a way to signal a passing _____ .
<u>NOUN</u>

MAD LIBS® is fun to play with friends, but you can also play it by yourself! To begin with, DO NOT look at the story on the page below. Fill in the blanks on this page with the words called for. Then, using the words you have selected, fill in the blank spaces in the story.

Now you've created your own hilarious MAD LIBS® game!

EVERYONE NEEDS
A GOOD FRIEND

_____ ADVERB

_____ NOUN

_____ ADJECTIVE

_____ ADJECTIVE

_____ ADJECTIVE

_____ PLURAL NOUN

_____ COLOR

_____ PLURAL NOUN

_____ VERB

_____ NOUN

_____ NOUN

_____ PLURAL NOUN

As a Greek philosopher _____ once said, "One good
                              ADVERB

_____ makes a poor man rich." Here are some important
     NOUN

qualities to look for in a/an _____ friend:
                                ADJECTIVE

• Whether you're right or _____ , your friend will be there
                              ADJECTIVE

for you—through thick and _____ .
                               ADJECTIVE

• When you are down in the _____ and feeling _____ ,
                              PLURAL NOUN   COLOR

your friend will tell you funny _____ to make you
                                     PLURAL NOUN

_____ with laughter.
     VERB

• When you don't have a/an _____ to wear, your friend
                              NOUN

should generously offer you their favorite _____ so you can
                                               NOUN

look like a million _____ .
                       PLURAL NOUN

PEACE, LOVE, AND POETRY

PLURAL NOUN _____

PERSON IN ROOM _____

VERB _____

NOUN _____

PLURAL NOUN _____

ADJECTIVE _____

PLURAL NOUN _____

NOUN _____

COLOR _____

PART OF THE BODY _____

VERB _____

NOUN _____

PLURAL NOUN _____

ADVERB _____

A PLACE _____

MAD LIBS® is fun to play with friends, but you can also play it by yourself! To begin with, DO NOT look at the story on the page below. Fill in the blanks on this page with the words called for. Then, using the words you have selected, fill in the blank spaces in the story.

Now you've created your own hilarious MAD LIBS® game!

MAD LIBS
PEACE, LOVE, AND POETRY

"Peace, Love, and the Pursuit of _____"
                                         PLURAL NOUN

by _____
        PERSON IN ROOM

Teach everyone you meet to _____ in perfect harmony,
                                         VERB

Reach out and embrace a friend or _____, or go hug a tree!
                                              NOUN

Preach to _____, both big and _____, to give
              PLURAL NOUN   ADJECTIVE

peace a chance,

And stop and smell the _____, or do a little dance. Love
                              PLURAL NOUN

your neighbors, love your friends, love your _____ , too—
                                                        NOUN

And love the good ol' USA—the red, the _____, and the blue!
                                                  COLOR

Extend your _____ in friendship to everyone you meet.
                 PART OF THE BODY

Invite a stranger to _____ , or bring a stray _____
                            VERB   NOUN

home to eat.

These random acts of _____ will put a smile on a face,
                              PLURAL NOUN

And they'll _____ transform (the) _____ into
                  ADVERB   A PLACE

a better place!

MAD LIBS® is fun to play with friends, but you can also play it by yourself! To begin with, DO NOT look at the story on the page below. Fill in the blanks on this page with the words called for. Then, using the words you have selected, fill in the blank spaces in the story.

Now you've created your own hilarious MAD LIBS® game!

TIE-DYE FOR FASHION

ADJECTIVE _____

ADJECTIVE _____

NOUN _____

ADJECTIVE _____

NOUN _____

PLURAL NOUN _____

PLURAL NOUN _____

PART OF THE BODY (PLURAL) _____

NOUN _____

ADJECTIVE _____

NUMBER _____

TYPE OF LIQUID _____

NOUN _____

ADJECTIVE _____

PART OF THE BODY (PLURAL) _____

MAD LIBS
TIE-DYE FOR FASHION

Tie-dying is a/an _____ way to dye your clothing so you can

ADJECTIVE

look like a/an _____ hippie. Here are some instructions for

ADJECTIVE

tie-dying your own _____ :

NOUN

1. Select a/an _____ article of clothing and use _____

ADJECTIVE NOUN

bands to tie it into different sections.

2. Prepare your dye according to the _____ on the package.

PLURAL NOUN

3. Remember to put on a pair of rubber _____ over your

PLURAL NOUN

_____ to protect them as you dip the _____

PART OF THE BODY (PLURAL) NOUN

into the dye.

4. For _____ results, keep the material in the dye for at

ADJECTIVE

least _____ minutes. Then remove and rinse under cold

NUMBER

running _____ .

TYPE OF LIQUID

5. Hang on a/an _____ outside to dry.

NOUN

6. Wear it and enjoy the _____ looks on people's

ADJECTIVE

_____ .

PART OF THE BODY (PLURAL)

MAD LIBS® is fun to play with friends, but you can also play it by yourself! To begin with, DO NOT look at the story on the page below. Fill in the blanks on this page with the words called for. Then, using the words you have selected, fill in the blank spaces in the story.

Now you've created your own hilarious MAD LIBS® game!

YOUR GOOD FORTUNE

PERSON IN ROOM (FEMALE) _____

NOUN _____

VERB _____

PART OF THE BODY _____

NOUN _____

PLURAL NOUN _____

PERSON IN ROOM (MALE) _____

CELEBRITY (MALE) _____

NOUN _____

A PLACE _____

ADJECTIVE _____

ADVERB _____

PLURAL NOUN _____

VERB ENDING IN "ING" _____

ADJECTIVE _____

ADJECTIVE _____

ADJECTIVE _____

PART OF THE BODY (PLURAL) _____

NOUN _____

MAD LIBS
YOUR GOOD FORTUNE

When I entered the room, Madame _____ , the
                                    PERSON IN ROOM (FEMALE)

famous _____ -teller, gestured for me to _____ .
            NOUN   VERB

"What do you wish to know?" she asked as she prepared to read my

_____ . "Will I marry a handsome _____ ?" I
    PART OF THE BODY   NOUN

asked. She replied, "Yes. Two _____ named _____
                                    PLURAL NOUN   PERSON IN ROOM (MALE)

and _____ think you are the prettiest, smartest _____
        CELEBRITY (MALE)   NOUN

in all of (the) _____ . Only one will make you truly _____ ,
                    A PLACE   ADJECTIVE

so you must choose _____ ." "Will I be successful?" I asked. "You
                        ADVERB

will find fame and _____ with your _____
                        PLURAL NOUN   VERB ENDING IN "ING"

skills," she responded. "But will I be happy?" "Yes, you will always be

surrounded by a/an _____ family and _____
                        ADJECTIVE   ADJECTIVE

friends who will put you on a/an _____ pedestal and worship
                                        ADJECTIVE

at your _____ ." *Wow*, I thought. *All that and she hasn't*
            PART OF THE BODY (PLURAL)

used her crystal _____ *yet!*
                        NOUN

MAD LIBS® is fun to play with friends, but you can also play it by yourself! To begin with, DO NOT look at the story on the page below. Fill in the blanks on this page with the words called for. Then, using the words you have selected, fill in the blank spaces in the story.

Now you've created your own hilarious MAD LIBS® game!

HALL MONITOR

_____ PERSON IN ROOM

_____ NOUN

_____ ADJECTIVE

_____ NOUN

_____ VERB ENDING IN "ING"

_____ ADJECTIVE

_____ ADJECTIVE

_____ NOUN

_____ NOUN

_____ ADJECTIVE

_____ ARTICLE OF CLOTHING

_____ VERB ENDING IN "ING"

_____ NOUN

_____ TYPE OF FOOD

_____ PLURAL NOUN

_____ VERB

_____ NOUN

MAD LIBS®
HALL MONITOR

My name is _____ . I'm the _____ monitor
PERSON IN ROOM · NOUN

and peacekeeper here at _____ _____
ADJECTIVE · NOUN

Memorial School. It's my duty to keep the students _____
VERB ENDING IN "ING"

through the halls in a/an _____ and orderly fashion.
ADJECTIVE

Originally, I wasn't sure I was _____ enough for this job.
ADJECTIVE

I'm not the strongest _____ in school, and I don't claim to
NOUN

be the smartest _____, either. But I have the _____
NOUN · ADJECTIVE

ability to sense that someone has something up his _____.
ARTICLE OF CLOTHING

So heed this warning: If you're thinking about _____ in
VERB ENDING IN "ING"

the hallways without a/an _____ pass or planning to start an
NOUN

all-out _____ fight in the cafeteria, forget about it. I have
TYPE OF FOOD

_____ in the back of my head. You can run, but you can't
PLURAL NOUN

_____ , and you'll be in the principal's _____
VERB · NOUN

in no time flat.

MAD LIBS® is fun to play with friends, but you can also play it by yourself! To begin with, DO NOT look at the story on the page below. Fill in the blanks on this page with the words called for. Then, using the words you have selected, fill in the blank spaces in the story.

Now you've created your own hilarious MAD LIBS® game!

FAMOUS HIPPIES IN HISTORY

ADJECTIVE _____

A PLACE _____

VERB _____

PLURAL NOUN _____

PERSON IN ROOM (MALE) _____

ADJECTIVE _____

PLURAL NOUN _____

ADJECTIVE _____

PLURAL NOUN _____

PERSON IN ROOM (FEMALE) _____

PLURAL NOUN _____

ADJECTIVE _____

ADJECTIVE _____

PLURAL NOUN _____

NOUN _____

PERSON IN ROOM (FEMALE) _____

NOUN _____

PLURAL NOUN _____

ADJECTIVE _____

NOUN _____

MAD LIBS®
FAMOUS HIPPIES IN HISTORY

The hippie lifestyle may be a thing of the past, but many _____
ADJECTIVE

hippies made (the) _____ a better place in which to live,
A PLACE

work, and _____. Here's a look at a few of those
VERB

_____ of the 1960s:
PLURAL NOUN

• **Barefoot** _____ was a/an _____ songwriter
PERSON IN ROOM (MALE)   ADJECTIVE

who wrote about love and _____. His _____
PLURAL NOUN   ADJECTIVE

music inspired millions of _____ everywhere.
PLURAL NOUN

• **Crazy Daisy** _____ was known for weaving beautiful
PERSON IN ROOM (FEMALE)

_____ into her hair. This _____ flower
PLURAL NOUN   ADJECTIVE

child also painted many _____ murals depicting
ADJECTIVE

_____ living in peace and _____.
PLURAL NOUN   NOUN

• **Grandma Groovy Pants** _____ was an anti-
PERSON IN ROOM (FEMALE)

_____ activist who championed equality for all
NOUN

_____ in our society and supported her _____
PLURAL NOUN   ADJECTIVE

beliefs by marching for justice and _____.
NOUN

THE SUMMER OF LOVE LETTERS, PART 1

PLURAL NOUN _____

ADJECTIVE _____

PLURAL NOUN _____

ADJECTIVE _____

ADJECTIVE _____

ADVERB _____

PLURAL NOUN _____

ADJECTIVE _____

PART OF THE BODY _____

ADVERB _____

A PLACE _____

ADJECTIVE _____

NOUN _____

PLURAL NOUN _____

ADJECTIVE _____

ADJECTIVE _____

PERSON IN ROOM (FEMALE) _____

MAD LIBS® is fun to play with friends, but you can also play it by yourself! To begin with, DO NOT look at the story on the page below. Fill in the blanks on this page with the words called for. Then, using the words you have selected, fill in the blank spaces in the story.

Now you've created your own hilarious MAD LIBS® game!

I was in the attic going through some old _____ when, to
                                                PLURAL NOUN

my _____ surprise, I came across my parents' old love
          ADJECTIVE

_____ . Here's one of Mom's most _____ letters:
      PLURAL NOUN   ADJECTIVE

My _____ Hippie Man,
          ADJECTIVE

I miss you _____—more than _____ can say! I
              ADVERB   PLURAL NOUN

miss your _____ smile. I miss the way my _____
              ADJECTIVE   PART OF THE BODY

beats when your eyes stare _____ into mine. I miss going for
                                  ADVERB

long walks at (the) _____ at sunset. Do you ever picture us
                        A PLACE

spending the rest of our _____ lives together? I do. I dream
                              ADJECTIVE

of our living in a cozy house with a picket _____ . I know in
                                                  NOUN

my heart of _____ that I want to grow _____
                PLURAL NOUN   ADJECTIVE

with you.

With all my _____ love,
                ADJECTIVE

_____
      PERSON IN ROOM (FEMALE)

MAD LIBS® is fun to play with friends, but you can also play it by yourself! To begin with, DO NOT look at the story on the page below. Fill in the blanks on this page with the words called for. Then, using the words you have selected, fill in the blank spaces in the story.

Now you've created your own hilarious MAD LIBS® game!

THE SUMMER OF LOVE
LETTERS, PART 2

_____ ADJECTIVE

_____ ADJECTIVE

_____ PLURAL NOUN

_____ NOUN

_____ PLURAL NOUN

_____ ADJECTIVE

_____ PART OF THE BODY

_____ PART OF THE BODY

_____ NOUN

_____ PART OF THE BODY

_____ NOUN

_____ PART OF THE BODY

_____ NOUN

_____ SILLY WORD

_____ NOUN

_____ ADVERB

_____ NOUN

_____ PERSON IN ROOM (MALE)

Now, here's a/an _____ letter from my _____
                      ADJECTIVE   ADJECTIVE

dad to my mom:

To the girl of my _____,
                    PLURAL NOUN

Not a/an _____ goes by that I don't think of you. I don't know
            NOUN

what I did to deserve you, but I thank my lucky _____ that
                                                    PLURAL NOUN

I am so _____ to be the one who holds the key to your
          ADJECTIVE

_____. I dreamed last night that I asked your father for your
PART OF THE BODY

_____ in marriage. With a/an _____ on his
PART OF THE BODY   NOUN

face, he nodded his _____ and said, "Yes." When I awakened, I
                      PART OF THE BODY

realized I don't want to wait until I graduate from _____ school.
                                                        NOUN

I want to come home now, drop down on one _____, put
                                              PART OF THE BODY

a diamond _____ on your finger, and pop the question. When
            NOUN

you say "_____" you'll make me the happiest _____
           SILLY WORD   NOUN

in the world.

Truly, madly, _____ in love with you,
                ADVERB

Your _____-to-be, _____
        NOUN   PERSON IN ROOM (MALE)

MAD LIBS® is fun to play with friends, but you can also play it by yourself! To begin with, DO NOT look at the story on the page below. Fill in the blanks on this page with the words called for. Then, using the words you have selected, fill in the blank spaces in the story.

Now you've created your own hilarious MAD LIBS® game!

TEAM PEACE

_____ NOUN

_____ PLURAL NOUN

_____ ADJECTIVE

_____ PERSON IN ROOM

_____ PLURAL NOUN

_____ ADJECTIVE

_____ PLURAL NOUN

_____ ADJECTIVE

_____ VERB

_____ ADJECTIVE

_____ PLURAL NOUN

_____ NOUN

_____ ADJECTIVE

_____ ADJECTIVE

_____ ADJECTIVE

_____ PART OF THE BODY

_____ NOUN

_____ ADJECTIVE

MAD LIBS
TEAM PEACE

It was the day of the most important _____ on the schedule
                                         NOUN

and the coach knew his team was a bundle of _____. He
                                              PLURAL NOUN

wisely invited the _____ Guru _____ to help
                       ADJECTIVE   PERSON IN ROOM

his players find their inner _____. The Guru's pep talk was
                                PLURAL NOUN

simple and _____:
               ADJECTIVE

Block out the screaming _____ in the stadium. Focus on
                            PLURAL NOUN

becoming one with the _____ ball. The most important thing is
                          ADJECTIVE

to believe you can _____ better today than you have in any
                       VERB

other _____ game this season. The opposing _____
          ADJECTIVE   PLURAL NOUN

will try to shake your _____ , but you must stay calm, cool,
                          NOUN

and _____ , and always be positive. If one of your teammates
        ADJECTIVE

makes a/an _____ play, give him a/an _____
               ADJECTIVE   ADJECTIVE

pat of encouragement on the _____ . Now put your
                                PART OF THE BODY

_____ faces on and go make us _____ !
    NOUN   ADJECTIVE

MAD LIBS® is fun to play with friends, but you can also play it by yourself! To begin with, DO NOT look at the story on the page below. Fill in the blanks on this page with the words called for. Then, using the words you have selected, fill in the blank spaces in the story.

Now you've created your own hilarious MAD LIBS® game!

GARAGE BAND DEBUT

_____ TYPE OF LIQUID

_____ PART OF THE BODY

_____ NOUN

_____ ADJECTIVE

_____ PART OF THE BODY (PLURAL)

_____ PLURAL NOUN

_____ NOUN

_____ ADJECTIVE

_____ COLOR

_____ PERSON IN ROOM

_____ PERSON IN ROOM

_____ ADVERB

_____ ADJECTIVE

_____ NUMBER

_____ ADVERB

_____ PLURAL NOUN

_____ PART OF THE BODY

_____ NOUN

_____ ADJECTIVE

MAD LIBS®
GARAGE BAND DEBUT

As the lights dimmed, I could feel beads of _____
                                                    TYPE OF LIQUID

drip down my _____. The school dance was my band's first
                  PART OF THE BODY

real _____ and I was so _____ , I was
          NOUN   ADJECTIVE

sure everyone could see my _____ shaking. "Hello,
                              PART OF THE BODY (PLURAL)

_____!" I shouted into the micro-_____.
   PLURAL NOUN   NOUN

"We're really happy to be here at your _____ dance. Tonight,
                                            ADJECTIVE

our first song will be '_____ Haze.'" I glanced back at
                              COLOR

_____ on keyboards and _____ on drums
   PERSON IN ROOM   PERSON IN ROOM

(both of whom were sweating _____), took a/an
                                    ADVERB

_____ breath, and began the count: "And a one, and a two,
   ADJECTIVE

and a one, two, _____!" The next thing I knew, the audience
                    NUMBER

was cheering _____ and dancing like _____. Even
                  ADVERB   PLURAL NOUN

the principal was tapping his _____ on the _____.
                                  PART OF THE BODY   NOUN

Who knows? A school dance tonight—maybe a/an _____
                                                    ADJECTIVE

record deal tomorrow!

From PEACE, LOVE, AND MAD LIBS® • Copyright © 2009 by Price Stern Sloan,
an imprint of Penguin Group (USA) Inc., 345 Hudson Street, New York, NY 10014.

DID YOU EVER HAVE ONE OF THOSE DAYS?

ADJECTIVE _____

NOUN _____

ADJECTIVE _____

VERB ENDING IN "ING" _____

NUMBER _____

ADJECTIVE _____

NOUN _____

NOUN _____

LETTER OF THE ALPHABET _____

ADJECTIVE _____

ADJECTIVE _____

EXCLAMATION _____

NOUN _____

MAD LIBS® is fun to play with friends, but you can also play it by yourself! To begin with, DO NOT look at the story on the page below. Fill in the blanks on this page with the words called for. Then, using the words you have selected, fill in the blank spaces in the story.

Now you've created your own hilarious MAD LIBS® game!

Dear Diary: What a/an _____ day! I forgot my gym
                        ADJECTIVE

_____ , so the _____ teacher made me do
      NOUN   ADJECTIVE

one hundred _____ jacks. I was late getting to homeroom
              VERB ENDING IN "ING"

and the teacher had me write _____ times, "I promise not to be
                                    NUMBER

_____ ever again." As if *that's* not enough, I was in the
   ADJECTIVE

bathroom and dropped my report in the _____! I can't turn in
                                              NOUN

a soaking wet _____ , so I'm probably going to get a/an
                   NOUN

_____ . Did I mention someone spilled a bowl of
   LETTER OF THE ALPHABET

_____ soup all over me at lunch? And worse than that, I bit
   ADJECTIVE

into an apple and cracked the filling in my _____ molar.
                                                ADJECTIVE

_____! I guess I just got up on the wrong side of the
   EXCLAMATION

_____ this morning.
      NOUN

MAD LIBS® is fun to play with friends, but you can also play it by yourself! To begin with, DO NOT look at the story on the page below. Fill in the blanks on this page with the words called for. Then, using the words you have selected, fill in the blank spaces in the story.

Now you've created your own hilarious MAD LIBS® game!

HIPPIE SPEAK, PART 1

ADJECTIVE _____

PLURAL NOUN _____

PERSON IN ROOM _____

NOUN _____

NUMBER _____

ADJECTIVE _____

PERSON IN ROOM _____

ADJECTIVE _____

PART OF THE BODY _____

PLURAL NOUN _____

PLURAL NOUN _____

ADJECTIVE _____

ADJECTIVE _____

VERB (PAST TENSE) _____

A PLACE _____

MAD LIBS®
HIPPIE SPEAK, PART 1

In addition to their distinctive style of dressing, hippies had their

own _____ language. Here are some of the most popular
      ADJECTIVE

_____:
  PLURAL NOUN

- **Groovy** meant cool. *That _____ is one groovy _____!*
          PERSON IN ROOM   NOUN

- **Far out** was _____ times better than *groovy. My mom's*
         NUMBER

  letting me go to the _____ concert with _____.
             ADJECTIVE   PERSON IN ROOM

  Far out!

- To **dig it** meant to understand. *When my teacher asked if I understood the*

  _____ homework, I nodded my _____ and
      ADJECTIVE   PART OF THE BODY

  said, "I dig it."

- **Threads** referred to clothing. *"Man, between her peace sign _____*
                         PLURAL NOUN

  and her tie-dyed _____, she's got really _____ threads!"
          PLURAL NOUN   ADJECTIVE

- If something was **a gas**, it meant you had a really _____
                            ADJECTIVE

  time. *It was a gas when we _____ with our friends at (the)*
                VERB (PAST TENSE)

  _____.
  A PLACE

MAD LIBS® is fun to play with friends, but you can also play it by yourself! To begin with, DO NOT look at the story on the page below. Fill in the blanks on this page with the words called for. Then, using the words you have selected, fill in the blank spaces in the story.

Now you've created your own hilarious MAD LIBS® game!

HIPPIE SPEAK, PART 2

NOUN _____

PERSON IN ROOM _____

ADJECTIVE _____

ADJECTIVE _____

NOUN _____

A PLACE _____

NOUN _____

ADJECTIVE _____

ADJECTIVE _____

PERSON IN ROOM _____

ADJECTIVE _____

NOUN _____

ADJECTIVE _____

PLURAL NOUN _____

PART OF THE BODY (PLURAL) _____

NOUN _____

MAD LIBS
HIPPIE SPEAK, PART 2

- Your **pad** was your home, or the place where you hung your

  _____. *Let's go hang out at* _____*'s pad and*
          NOUN   PERSON IN ROOM

  listen to some _____ *be-bop.*
                         ADJECTIVE

- To **crash** meant to sleep. *You look* _____. *Why don't you*
                                                ADJECTIVE

  go in the bedroom and crash on the _____?
                                              NOUN

- When you **split**, you left (the) _____. *As soon as the*
                                            A PLACE

  _____ *rang, we split from school and went shopping*
         NOUN

  for _____ *threads.*
              ADJECTIVE

- **The scene** referred to a place where something _____
                                                            ADJECTIVE

  was going on. *If* _____ *is in the principal's office, it*
                      PERSON IN ROOM

  must be alan _____ *scene.*
                     ADJECTIVE

- **Happening** described a place where every _____ was
                                                      NOUN

  having fun. *Between the* _____ *music and the delicious*
                                  ADJECTIVE

  _____, *that party was happening!*
     PLURAL NOUN

- **Peace out** meant good-bye. *He held up two* _____
                                                  PART OF THE BODY (PLURAL)

  as he left the _____ *and said, "Peace out."*
                        NOUN